QUEENS
OF EUROPE

QUEENS OF EUROPE

OLYMPIQUE LYONNAIS FÉMININ

ABDULLAH ABDULLAH

First published by Pitch Publishing, 2021

Pitch Publishing
A2 Yeoman Gate
Yeoman Way
Worthing
Sussex
BN13 3QZ
www.pitchpublishing.co.uk
info@pitchpublishing.co.uk

ISBN 978 1 78531 845 0

Typesetting and origination by Pitch Publishing
Printed and bound in India by Replika Press Pvt. Ltd.

Contents

Dedication

To my family and friends that have
supported this endeavour from the
start and to the small group of Twitter
followers that have appreciated my
work from day one. Thank you for
your support.

Foreword

IN 2017, after England won the Women's Cricket World Cup, beating India in dramatic style at Lord's, the sportswriter Emma John wrote a piece in *The Guardian* asking: 'Where are all the books about women in sport?'

That year was a memorable one for women's sport: there was a UEFA Women's Euro hosted and won by Holland in front of record attendances, a Cricket World Cup and an Athletics World Championships in England, and a record-breaking Women's Rugby World Cup in Ireland.

In her piece Emma reflected on how women's sport had been making more and more headlines, media coverage had been rising, and continues to climb, as had viewing figures, but there remained an absence of books about these headline-making athletes.

Two years later, in 2019, the same sort of 'game-changing summer' was heralded. The FIFA Women's

World Cup in France was the central piece in this historic year for women's sport.

FIFA estimated that one billion people watched the tournament and individual viewership records were broken in the UK, France, China, Germany, Brazil and the US.

There were also records broken on the pitch. The USWNT recorded the highest margin of victory in a World Cup game in their 13-0 win over Thailand and Brazilian legend Marta became the leading scorer at a men's or women's World Cup, taking her tally to a staggering 17 goals.

Unfortunately, history has told us that if you just sit back and wait for stories like those to be told, they will likely be forgotten.

It's one of the reasons I wanted to work in sports journalism. As a young girl who was obsessed with football, I found it really strange that women's footballers rarely featured in the magazines I subscribed to or on television, bar the odd sighting of Rachel Yankey and Kelly Smith.

As I got older, I learnt more about inequalities in sport, wrote a dissertation on sexism in football and started working for the gender equality charity Women in Sport. I wanted to be part of the change and ensure that these women and their accomplishments wouldn't be forgotten.

Olympique Lyonnais Féminin is certainly a team that should live long in the memory of football fans and be etched in the history books.

The story of Lyon and their rise to dominance is akin to many sporting dynasties that have become folklore throughout football. Real Madrid's *Galácticos*, the Busby Babes, the Lisbon Lions and countless other teams have been immortalised through literature, with pages and pages dedicated to their achievements and their legacy.

It's shocking that this is the first book to be written about a team that has won the UEFA Women's Champions League seven times and the French league title 14 times in a row.

It is a remarkable rise to dominance and a story that needs to be shared with football fans around the world, and Abdullah is the perfect person to do that. He has an unrivalled tactical eye and an in-depth knowledge of the women's game, and he has (virtually) scoured the globe to interview some of the world's biggest players and legends of Olympique Lyonnais.

I first came across Abdullah's work because he kept tagging me in posts about his articles on Twitter! His pestering eventually paid off because I dived into the work he was doing on Total Football Analysis.

11

His work is unique, with deep tactical dives into women's teams, players and coaches, content that you rarely find anywhere else. He has an amazing eye for tactical detail and incorporates stats to bring breadth and depth to his work; rather than just plonking them in a piece as a distraction, they're embedded throughout.

Abdullah tells the story of Lyon's rise through the lens of tactics, players and positions, while also looking at the story off the pitch that propelled Lyon to greatness.

I can't think of any books about women's football or even women's sport like this one. A first of its kind and a fantastic read.

I'm excited to see what's next for Abdullah and the teams and stories he's going to continue to shine a light on.

Florence Lloyd-Hughes

Introduction

'If you are grateful, I will surely increase you (in favour)' – Qur'an 14:7

IN TRUTH, writing at all was never on the cards for me, let alone as a career or hobby. I never took a real interest in writing anything until my late 20s and that was only when I found myself knocking at the door of Ronnie Dog Media and Chris Darwen.

I discovered women's football when Total Football Analysis covered the 2019 FIFA Women's World Cup and through the luck of the draw, I was handed France. We finished the tournament and it was there that I decided to dedicate my time to writing women's football analysis for the site. From the Women's Super League to Division 1 Féminine, I delved into a whole new world of teams, players and personalities which in truth was difficult at first, but slowly became the norm. After a year of writing and gaining experience, I decided to bring women's football tactics to a wider audience and it is from here where this book was born.

Olympique Lyonnais Féminin was the perfect place to start given their status in the game. I am a fan first, but the storyline was perfect – the most successful team in European history on the verge of equalling Real Madrid's record. This prompted me to take a closer look at their tactics. I fell in love with the side after watching them stomp away teams in the UEFA Women's Champions League. One by one, they swept teams aside with their swashbuckling style. The peak was their 4-1 victory over Barcelona in the 2018 UEFA Women's Champions League Final, and in that moment they were the Queens of Europe once again. The premise of this book is to show you the tactical concepts that have made them such an unstoppable force, but also the work that has gone in behind the glitz and glamour.

The network I've built over the last 12 to 18 months has been astonishing and I've been privileged to speak to some fascinating minds in the game. This book has given me the opportunity to reach people I didn't think would ever be possible. There are a few individuals to thank, but firstly I'd like to thank my family for their support in this endeavour, even if they don't understand the contents of my work.

A big thanks to Ada Hegerberg, Jess Fishlock and Katriina Talaslahti for their insights into the club, and for their time in sitting and chatting with me about all things football and Lyon. Thanks to the intellectual Flo Lloyd-Hughes for being a helping hand in the process and Sid Lowe for his time and opinion. American superfan Arianna Scavetti gave me a better understanding of the team over the years and provided a detailed insight into the side from a fan's perspective.

There are a few individuals at Total Football Analysis, past and present, that can't be overlooked. Chris Darwen, the brains behind the TFA operations, for giving me a platform to write on and pushing me further; Lee Scott for his direction and feedback in the early days which helped shape my work; Dániel Garai, Lorihanna Shushkova, Ryan McCready, Gavin Robertson, Sathish Prasad, Ravshan Ergashev and Jamie Brackpool, all of whom have had an impact on my writing and analysis. I can't thank them enough.

Craig Megson, a long-time friend and pre-Carlo Ancelotti Everton supporter, gets a special mention. It was he who introduced me to tactics and Football Manager and made me obsessed with wanting to learn more. There were all these nights spent driving around the streets of Sharjah talking about Chelsea, Everton, Lyon and Real Madrid, to name a few.

Last but not least, I need to thank two individuals whose support and help has been relentless. Andrew Flint and Domagoj Kostanjšak are two gents that taught me so much early on and helped me grow. Andrew, for being my mentor when I first started writing, and Domagoj, for keeping me on track and forcing me to level up every time I sat back in my comfort zone. He's the man I can bounce ideas off whether it be 7pm or 4am. Smaldini's Venting Room finally has its shining moment.

I hope you enjoy reading this book as much as I enjoyed writing it, and come out with a better understanding of why Olympique Lyon Féminin are Queens of Europe.

Chapter 1

Building a Dynasty

AS THE sun rose over the Anoeta Stadium in San Sebastián on 30 August 2020, there was a feeling of curiosity and intrigue that set the mood in Spain that day. This was indeed the day of the final of the UEFA Women's Champions League, between Olympique Lyonnais Féminin and VfL Wolfsburg. Whoever won the European title that day would in their own right set a new precedent and story for years to come. The feeling at the time was that this was the year that Lyon could be dethroned …

* * *

History has told us many stories about teams that have dominated leagues and competitions for long spells. From club teams to international outfits, football is littered with an array of tales recalling how dynasties were built. You have Real Madrid's *Galácticos* from the early 2000s, winning 11 titles over eight years with a team built on superstars. Next, you could look at Arrigo Sachi's trophy-winning AC Milan machine, which won an unprecedented 16 trophies between 1988 and 1994. Then there's the early 1990s to 2013 period, when Sir Alex Ferguson's Manchester United could be deemed as the most dominant side in modern footballing history with UEFA Champions League and English Premier League titles galore. What makes this achievement even more impressive was his ability to do it with different teams built over that period. His ability to create, utilise and rebuild was remarkable.

There are a host of other teams who have built a legacy in a similar fashion, such as Barcelona, Ajax and Arsenal, but one common factor between all of them is the dynasty they've built. In the midst of all of their success, there is one team that has flown under the radar despite having risen and garnered countless titles while being so utterly dominant since their very inception that there has been no sign of stopping: they are Olympique Lyonnais Féminin.

Olympique Lyonnais Féminin have taken women's football by storm and crushed all those who have appeared before them. Although there hasn't been a real contender to the throne, their performances are still worthy of praise. All you have to do is look back at their achievements since their inception and see what they've accomplished. Seven UEFA Women's Champions League, 14 Division 1 Féminine and nine Coupe de France Féminine titles is no small feat considering their first title came two years after their revival in the 2006/07 season. The numbers speak for themselves, but to truly understand their dominance, one must look deeper into what's made them such a commanding unit. It goes beyond signing superstars and nurturing talent; the success of any organisation comes from within, and Lyon is no exception.

People know of Lyon's men's team, who have an infamous reputation for nurturing prestigious talents and selling them on for exorbitant amounts. From Karim Benzema and Michael Essien from yesteryear to bringing up the next generation in Houssem Aouar and Rayan Cherki, the production line of talent doesn't seem to stop. This all comes down to the vision of Jean-Michel Aulas, the owner and president of the football club Olympique Lyonnais. While he was establishing the Lyon men's team with back-to-back domestic title wins, Aulas wanted to create a women's team under the same banner, although this time he had a different plan. He wanted to create the equivalent to his own super team, dripping with the best superstars on the planet

– his own *Galácticos*, or more appropriately, Queens of Europe.

This project began in 2004, when OL Groupe, the parent company that owns Olympique Lyon, bought out FC Lyon and rebranded them as Olympique Lyonnais Féminin. Since then, he's not let up on his promise, acquiring the services of Camille Abily, Megan Rapinoe, Alex Morgan, Hope Solo and Lucy Bronze, to name but a few, in the early stages. This resulted in their early successes in the UEFA Women's Champions League and Division 1 Féminine titles. The current squad is still equally full of illustrious talent, harbouring some of the best that women's football has to offer. The lure Lyon brings is second to none and is comparable to the pull Barcelona or Real Madrid have on the men's game. You just can't help yourself when they come calling.

To start with, you have Ada Hegerberg, the Norwegian striker who was the first female Ballon d'Or winner, and arguably the best striker in women's football over the last five years. Wendie Renard came through the youth set-up and has become one of the longest-serving members of the squad, and even moved on to be club captain. Dzsenifer Marozsán has over 100 caps for Germany and over 50 appearances for Lyon, and is easily considered one of the best creative attacking midfielders of her generation. Just looking at these three names, you begin to get a sense of the type of personalities that come through the club. From generational talents to homegrown youth products, this Lyon side has managed to balance development and ready-made purchases.

'A very important factor for us to continue being the best club in the world, we always need to look ourselves in the mirror trying to look at where we can improve year in, year out. That takes a lot of responsibility from us, the players, but [an improvement] in the direction of trying to improve in the way we think, recruit, and the long-term planning from the sporting director.' – Ada Hegerberg

Every year there is a need to reinforce the playing squad in the hope of eradicating complacency and keeping motivation high. Giving world-class players high-level competition keeps them on their toes and it pushes them to improve. In the last 12 months alone, they've brought in Sara Björk Gunnarsdóttir from VfL Wolfsburg and the young full-back pairing of Australian Ellie Carpenter and Montpellier's Sakina Karchaoui. While the latter two are young, up-and-coming players, Sara Björk came from a Wolfsburg side that has dominated the Frauen-Bundesliga. She continues the trend of top-class players in their prime making the move over to Lyon. The most recent transfer window just saw Nikita Parris make the move over from Manchester City, and she has settled well ever since.

The project needed financial backing, but most importantly, it needed to be treated as a priority – not an afterthought. This is where Aulas has truly stood out from the rest and why he's considered one of the best owners in world football. Possibly the one common factor that came through after speaking to some players was the social investment he's made in the team as much as the financial one. Ada Hegerberg, Jess Fishlock and Katriina Talaslahti were all very complimentary and passionate when it came to the president in this regard.

'I've never known anyone who is that committed or invested in his women's team. [Aulas] is a game-changer. He's a top leader and all the success comes from him because he had a vision.' – Ada Hegerberg

'When you see him, he's always lovely – you know that he cares. He's not a president that is far removed from the [day-to-day] operations. He flies to our games and gives us a pep talk for all the big games. He has spearheaded the men's, women's and youth teams, [which is] what makes it special really –

*he's just phenomenal. You don't feel like you're
miles away from the head of the organisation.'* –
Jess Fishlock

The first word that comes to mind when you read this
is respect. He acts and gives the women's team the same
privileges the men enjoy. This comes from the culture
he's instilled at the club. From attending matches and
giving team talks, to providing charter jets, VIP access
in and out of the airport, as well as six-figure salaries, he
has shown how a women's football team can operate and
set standards on the pitch if they're equally taken care of
off it. The outcome? A high-quality football team that
has achieved near-total European domination.

Aulas is one of the main instigators of Lyon's success
but more importantly he has fuelled the growth we see in
women's football today. Barcelona have started investing
more into their women's team, and their appearance in
the 2018/19 UEFA Women's Champions League Final
suggests they've come a long way. Paris Saint-Germain
are slowly but surely making strides by investing in
their playing squad, while the German giants of Bayern
Munich and Wolfsburg are edging closer through some
intricate tactical improvements.

However, the biggest strides are arguably coming
from the Women's Super League in England with the

boards of both Chelsea and Manchester City investing heavily in their women's teams. Under Gareth Taylor, Manchester City managed to sign Rose Lavelle, Sam Mewis and Lucy Bronze, while Chelsea prised away Sam Kerr, Pernille Harder and Melanie Leupolz from their respective clubs. This is being written before the start of the 2020/21 UEFA Women's Champions League, but it is believed that these two clubs will be Lyon's closest competitors in years. Speaking to Hegerberg, she echoes this sentiment and believes that this sort of investment is crucial not only for the longevity of women's football, but also keeping Lyon motivated.

> *'This is a huge factor for us to stay motivated. We depend on other clubs investing the same amount as Lyon to keep pushing. I hope other clubs take inspiration and motivation from it [the investment] because we're all in it and want to see it evolve. I think we have a big stake in this but even with the gap [closing], we won our fifth Champions League title.'* – Ada Hegerberg

Each member of the squad has been directly responsible for their trophy haul at some point over the past decade. Eugénie Le Sommer scored the opening goal of the 2019/20 UEFA Women's Champions League

Final, while Hegerberg scored a hat-trick in the final a season earlier against Barcelona. Bronze scored against Manchester City in 2018 to qualify them for the final that year. These superstars have delivered at a high level for years while other teams have chopped and changed their squads. The mixture of class and elegance is truly remarkable with key players remaining a constant in their success. Each of these players has done more than enough to earn the title of Queens of Europe.

Chapter 2

Formations, Systems and Build-up Structure

LOOKING AT Lyon's tactical concepts, it's important to break down and understand the different segments that create a coherent attacking unit. They've mostly followed a similar system over the last few years with a few tweaks when managers have come and gone. The playing style between Reynald Pedros and Jean-Luc Vasseur is similar, with no colossal changes in tactics, although Vasseur has brought his own flavours to the side. Other than different personnel combinations and tactical flexibility when it comes to playing higher-quality sides, for the most part, the 'Lyon' way of playing has been largely the same. The tactics can be split into three distinct phases: build-up play, middle-third transitions and final-third movements. All three phases have their own unique triggers and set of movements that integrate and marry players from different parts of the pitch to create a seamless flow of movement from one end of the pitch to the other.

For a better understanding of both their attacking and defensive mechanics, it's important to dissect their overall formation and system to better discern how it all integrates and pieces together. Lyon have traditionally been a team that have used a variety of formations, but in essence they are all very similar in terms of their desired output. On paper it looks like a 4-3-3, but during games, it morphs into a 4-2-3-1, 4-3-1-2 and 4-4-2 diamond system. The whole idea is to create a sort of flexible and unpredictable shape while retaining structural principles for both attacking and defending situations.

We'll break down each part of the team into 'units' – four defenders, three midfielders and three attackers. Each unit is responsible for almost all parts of their game when it comes to build-up, transitions, final-third movement and finishing. *Figure 1* (on page 28) is an illustration of Lyon's starting formation and how the movement of certain players can easily bring change. The numbers in different areas of the pitch give Lyon a numerical advantage when required. For example, if they start out with a 4-3-3 and move into a

4-1-2-1-2/4-4-2 diamond, then they are able to gain a numbers advantage which allows them extra players to progress the ball forward or counter-press if they give up possession in the central areas.

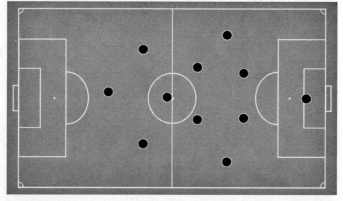

[FIGURE 1]

Lyon's approach has always been more possession-based, which is the crux and foundation of their ball progression methods. They are a side regimented in structure and organisation but with freedom of movement between positions from the back. The team's build-up tactics can be described as process-oriented, but there is enough flexibility in their way of working to change things up if the conventional methods are blocked, such as opting for a more direct approach. In essence, it's about ball progression through the thirds by inviting pressure and moving players out of position to create space, especially against rigid, more compact teams.

Lyon often come up against teams with a high capacity to utilise mid to low blocks to stop their attacking talents from wreaking havoc. Starting with the goalkeeper, Sarah Bouhaddi, Lyon will first and foremost find one of the two centre-backs as their initial point of contact. There are times when a defensive midfielder – mainly Saki Kumagai – will slot in between the two centre-backs – who push out wide – and become a third central defender in build-up in certain situations which creates numerical superiority, an additional build-up option and the trigger for both full-backs to push up. Regardless, once the ball reaches one of Griedge Mbock Bathy, Kadeisha Buchanan or Wendie Renard, their first priority is to go wide and find the full-backs. When the full-back pushes up, it triggers the near-sided central midfielder to slot into the full-back position. What this does is ensure that Lyon

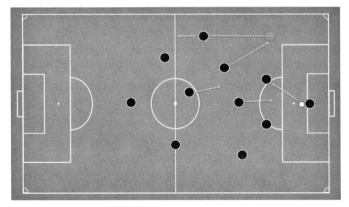

[FIGURE 2]

don't leave any gaps at the back and protect themselves against any turnovers in possession.

Taking a look at *Figure 2* (page 29), this is a clear representation of this concept, where the goalkeeper will look to find one of the two centre-halves. Once the pass is made, it triggers the near-sided full-back to start venturing forward and asks the defensive midfielder to slot in to fill in the vacant spaces. This then prompts movement from other players to move in closer to provide a passing option and always look to outnumber the opposition in that area of the pitch. They almost want to play the ball to the wide areas, bring it back inside in midfield, and in the final third, send it back out to the wide player to cross or run into the box. The whole idea is to create numerical superiority in the wide areas to allow for easier ball progression.

There is a big emphasis on involving different parts of the team in each phase of play and it's worth exploring how important the full-backs are in Lyon's system. They play an important role in build-up as the main outlet when it comes to ball progression, and must be tactically intelligent to understand the build-up and transition mechanics and be fast enough to move between these positions. In the final third, they provide an extra attacking option with their crossing if a cutback or inside pass isn't available.

These qualities make up the perfect Lyon full-back which has been seen in their recruitment over the years. Lucy Bronze is an impeccable example of the type of full-back they look to find: excellent in both the attacking and defending side of the game, but also with the speed to make up for any mishaps (if any) and the tactical intelligence to understand game situations and the intricate mechanics and triggers that come up. Though she is the quintessential role model for the position, players of a similar profile and quality are what Lyon are looking for across the board. If a player doesn't fit their system, she is moved on rather quickly.

The benefit of having a world-class centre-forward in Ada Hegerberg is her ability to be a dominant force in the air as well as a sly fox on the ground, which gives the full-backs a fixed target to aim for. Just like Bronze, Amel Majri set the standard for the left-back position for Lyon, and though she's been moved further forward in recent seasons, the left-backs that have followed are in her mould: strong, attacking players who have the capacity to create goalscoring opportunities. The acquisition of Sakina Karchaoui and Ellie Carpenter is a result of the standards Majri and Bronze have left. Both are young, attacking full-backs with the pace and raw potential to blossom into proficient talents.

When the ball reaches midfield, Lyon's build-up is reliant on off-the-ball movements from the players around them when in possession. It is here where they create passing opportunities by the use of triangles and third-man runs. Once you have a full-back in a position to move forward, you'll often find the second or third midfielder comes across to become the third man in support and execute passing triangle exchanges to play around the opposition players on that side. Dzsenifer Marozsán is important here as the number ten, whose movement not only adds an extra passing option but is perfect for evading the opposition's press in midfield, making her an excellent player on the ball in tight spaces. Amandine Henry is equally proficient in these spaces, and combined with the attacking nous of their full-backs and intelligent movement from the attackers, Lyon are able to move the ball effectively from this area into the half-spaces from where they will look to attack. From here, Lyon will play passes into the half-spaces or wide areas for runners like Henry, Cascarino and Le Sommer.

So how is it that Lyon can pack numbers into midfield? It's down to their flexible shape that enables them to become much more agile in and out of possession. The 4-3-3 will switch to a 4-4-2 or a diamond formation of sorts to give them greater midfield presence. Essentially, one winger will tuck into midfield while the other becomes a centre-forward and in a matter of seconds, Lyon have the numbers to execute the ball progression method. It's this collective movement of the ball that involves all three 'units' and ensures there are enough players around to deal with any outcome. A lot of what you'll notice about their midfield movements is that no player is ever static; instead, they want to be in space to both progress play and be on hand to fill in different positions once vacated. Typically, from here the wingers and strikers get involved and enter the final phase of play. This is all part of their positional rotations which will be explained in more detail, but it's important to note that this is a key component of their play.

Looking at *Figure 3* you'll notice the players' positioning in relation to the ball-carrier. Closer to the ball-carrier is an immediate passing option both to

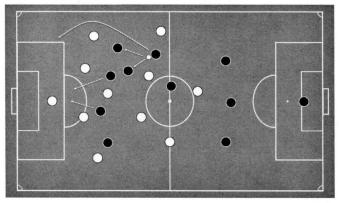

[FIGURE 3]

33

her left (a central midfielder) and in front (a winger), but instead of playing the obvious forward pass, the ball-carrier will play the ball infield and start making a forward run beyond the winger. The central midfielder who has the ball will now attempt a pass into the winger and at this point, the ball has progressed slightly farther, although the run from the initial ball-carrier, the full-back, has now opened up the opportunity to continue the attacking move by being in a more advanced passing position. Because of Lyon's constant changes in shape, they are able to bring in more players to the forward areas, with the right-winger moving into a centre-forward position along with the number ten.

Chapter 3

Role of the Sixes

IT COULD be argued that the central defensive midfielders are the most important pieces in the puzzle. The two deeper midfielders are responsible for more than just protecting the back four or providing attacking support, but are assigned multiple tasks. From filling in different positions defensively to providing a killer final pass in attacking situations, the two represent the engine to Lyon's myriad formidable attacking talents. They are involved in build-up by filling in for the full-backs as well as moving into more attacking positions to create overloads in midfield to again help ball progression. Additionally, they allow the more forward-thinking players the freedom to attack without really worrying about their defensive duties.

They will also have a say in the final third, with one of them providing support to increase the number of players available. The pair are a pendulum and bring balance to a side that could easily be top-heavy, so it's important for the relationship to be good with constant communication. If one pushes up, the other sits a bit deeper. It's this sort of understanding that is important, not only with these two players, but ingrained amongst the squad themselves. In the final third, the attacking midfielder, wingers and strikers will join in to progress the ball and play each other in through crosses and cutbacks. In a sense, this is how the team will move the ball from back to front with almost every player being involved, which brings up the point of player movement and positional changes.

The role of the six, or defensive midfielder, is extremely important. Not only do they play a role in build-up, but they influence the way Lyon attack. Over the years the role has seen a number of intelligent players being used and just the names alone are an indication of the quality of players needed to play there. Élise Bussaglia, Jess Fishlock and Sara Björk Gunnarsdóttir are standout names with differing roles, but their biggest success has arguably been Japanese international Saki Kumagai.

She has made the role her own since joining Lyon and has redefined it by bringing in a mix of defensive astuteness and intelligence on the ball. Capable of playing as a centre-back as well, Kumagai has the awareness and knowledge needed to know how the position should be played. The Lyon 'number six' needs to be able to protect the back four by carrying out the typical screening job but also needs to facilitate the advancing players such as the full-backs. The trigger for both full-backs to push forward comes when the defensive midfielder drops in between the two centre-backs.

In doing so, she adds a layer of protection and keeps the defence at a minimum of three, which acts as a catalyst in the middle and final third. This means both full-backs can maraud forward and become a bigger threat, as illustrated in *Figure 4*. As part of the ripple effect, the wingers will move into the half-spaces to allow the full-backs to push up as circulation outlets or counter-pressing options.

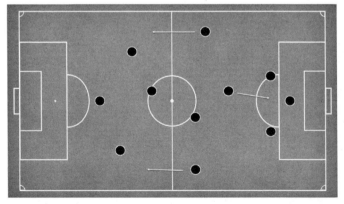

[FIGURE 4]

If Kumagai stays in midfield, it triggers one full-back to move up into an attacking position as mentioned already, while the other full-back comes inside and acts as a faux third central defender. The other central midfielder and attacking midfielder will stay in a more central position allowing the two wide players to create the width. Ultimately this creates an almost 3-2-5 formation allowing for a whole host of attacking options. If countered, one of the five will drop in immediately to support the two in midfield. *Figure 5* shows how this theoretically looks on the pitch. The central players will be on hand to stop any counter-attacks and the five forward players are there to overload the defending team. When you have two competent central midfielders who won't roam too far away from each other, then it creates a balance between attack and defence.

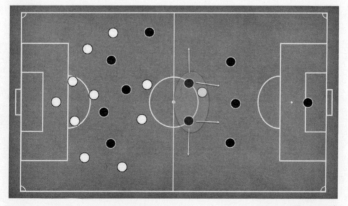

[*FIGURE 5*]

38

The other defensive midfielder is more of the connector or enabler of the side. Usually playing a box-to-box role, this entails a more supportive character at both ends of the pitch, with a bit more influence in the attacking half. This brings a balance between the two players, with one being a bit more defensive while the other is a bit more of an attacking presence.

Amandine Henry has played this role exceptionally well across both her stints and has become one of the best in her position. Her box-to-box style enables the side to have a balance of ball-carriers and off-the-ball runners. Henry can do both, which means that different attacking situations can be tackled differently. For example, Delphine Cascarino is a winger that prefers to carry the ball in attacking areas, so having someone like Henry around to link play and put Cascarino into a more attacking position makes it much easier. The role also requires the player to counter-press and act as the infield passing option when the full-backs first take the ball into midfield.

Overall, you can see how the two defensive midfielders play a key role in influencing the way Lyon have played their football. The 2019/20 season saw these two run riot in midfield playing at their commanding best with their complementary styles. The roles require spatial awareness, athleticism and most importantly game intelligence, with their effect evident throughout the phases of play.

Chapter 4

Positional Rotations and Final-Third Attacking Methods

BY THIS point, you'll have noticed that Lyon rely a lot on positional rotations, and that every player is not afraid of moving into an unfamiliar position, which is very reminiscent of the renowned concept of Total Football. While this isn't exactly that, Lyon implement a very good impression of a concept that has long been practised and instilled. Not many teams have been able to successfully execute it, with Pep Guardiola's Barcelona side coming close in recent times. Take the central midfield duo; when one moves, the other fills in, but this isn't limited to just players in a similar position. The concept is simple – players interchange positions to gain superiority in certain areas to ensure there are no gaps left around the pitch. Under their former coach

Pedros, the concept was very much a key component to his style of play, and that has continued under Vasseur. Seeing Marozsán slot into a defensive midfield position to pick up possession or Majri moving into a central midfield position are not uncommon sights. The full-backs will come infield and take up midfield positions when one pushes up to fill the void left there.

The idea is to counter-press and win back the ball with enough players around. It's this sort of intelligent movement and capability of pulling off something akin to Total Football – which in women's football is a rarity – that makes Lyon such a thrilling team to watch. In an attacking sense, Lyon use these rotations to create space in the final third, making it difficult for opposing defenders to mark and pick up players. If Hegerberg is marked, it means Eugénie Le Sommer or Majri are in space elsewhere, which is what makes them such a

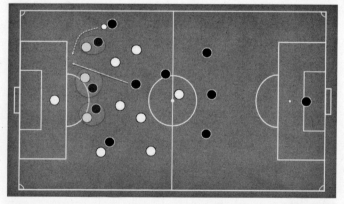

[FIGURE 6]

dangerous proposition. You'll notice this concept and how it plays a major role in how they operate on the pitch integrated throughout their tactical ideologies via the representation in *Figure 6*.

For the most part, Lyon want to progress the ball down the flanks to take advantage of their quick wide players. Their attacking quartet are equipped with the skills to play both centrally and wide, and though they aren't a side that intrinsically counter-attacks, the potential to do so is there. Lyon have attacking players who are able to carry out a variety of roles. Though they are specialists in their given positions, they are each able to fulfil different roles when asked to move into other positions. In doing so, the team is able to achieve complete positional rotations, which enables them to deceive the opposition and score goals. So, once the ball reaches the final third, how does the team look to penetrate and create goalscoring chances?

Generally speaking, Lyon use the wide areas to give more time to the central players to make their moves in the box. As seen before, their reliance on good off-the-ball movements is how they are able to create space and chances, and given they have some technically gifted and intelligent players in the forward areas, it makes sense to. Once the full-back and winger find their way into the final third, the idea is for one of them to find a good crossing position for the forwards inside the box. You'll find the striker, attacking midfielder and often the opposite winger or central midfielder making a run too, which gives Lyon a three- or four-player advantage. Given the late run from the midfielder from the deeper areas, Lyon have the element of surprise and unpredictability on their side. The typical cross can be either floated or whipped in, given that Hegerberg is proficient in the air and on the ground.

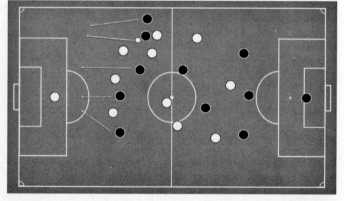

[FIGURE 7]

Figure 7 is an illustration of Lyon in the final third creating a goalscoring chance. You'll see the full-back in a narrow position in possession with the winger overlapping and the attacking midfielder in the half-space. The ball will be played into the path of the winger, prompting the attacking midfielder to make a run across into the box to meet an inevitable cross. One of the reasons Majri was moved into a more advanced role was because of her attacking forays and ability to come in late whether she's played in central midfield or on the left wing. Le Sommer plays as a second striker from the left-wing position and Marozsán excels in tight spaces, so they are good passing options on the edge of the box. The likes of Sara Björk Gunnarsdóttir and Henry will make late runs to the edge of the box and beyond, timing their runs to get on the end of a cutback or cross.

The 2019/20 season saw Lyon forced into a change in the striking department where Nikita Parris was deployed with Hegerberg out with an ACL injury. When Hegerberg starts she is a mobile focal point, who makes more vertical movements but does most of it in the final third. Parris is a much more eccentric centre-forward who wants to be constantly moving but is not a very imposing presence up front. More of a false nine, Parris is not a focal point but a facilitator who wants to use other players like Le Sommer much more. Lyon had to adapt slightly during the second half of the season, especially in the latter stages of the UEFA Women's Champions League, with more attempts through the middle. Using Marozsán's creativity and the inward movements of Majri and Le Sommer, they were able to give Parris more central passing options to execute some intricate passages of play. Often Lyon will morph into a 4-4-2 out of possession but this time used the 4-1-2-1-2 shape to gain a lot more central coverage and use the width from the full-backs more than before.

The end goal is the same: to get players in the box for crosses and cutbacks through rotations and overloads. Lyon do have a plan B, which uses their deeper central midfielders to play long balls over the top and has been seen in counter-attacking moves. Against Paris Saint-Germain in the league, there were a couple of times when Kumagai and Henry played long balls into the wide areas as soon as they received it from the centre-backs. This again highlights their unpredictable nature in the way they want to attack and build out from the back. The overarching attacking principles in this team haven't changed much over the years, which is remarkable given the stark improvements in women's football. Bayern Munich, Paris Saint-Germain and Wolfsburg fared much better in 2019/20 and made it more of a contest in Lyon's run to the title, but the tactics that have served them well for the past few years still held up.

Chapter 5

Defensive Shapes, Rotations and Transitions

THOUGH ONLY 4-3-3 by name, this formation regularly changes on the pitch as seen in an attacking sense. They've used a 4-1-4-1 and a 4-4-2 on occasion, rarely starting with them but rather opting for them as part of their free-flowing tactical changes within the game. They primarily rely on their superiority in possession to ensure they keep the opposition as far away from their goal as possible.

The 4-3-3 is comprised of two ball-playing centre-backs, two flying full-backs, two all-action defensive midfielders, a creative attacking number ten, two energetic wingers and one complete forward. The most important roles are those of the two defensive midfielders who are tasked with keeping the balance and shape of the team, regardless of how it changes. However, each position plays a vital role in the overall balance and functionality of the system, which has been Lyon's underlying principle for their tactics. Understanding the out-of-possession defensive shape shows us the foundation to Lyon's defensive structure. This chapter will go into detail on the two out-of-possession shapes Lyon utilise in the defensive phase that occur under different circumstances.

The first involves Lyon setting up in a 4-4-2 or 4-4-2 diamond shape (4-1-2-1-2), which is triggered once the opposition starts playing out from the back. The attacking midfielder or winger often joins the striker to create the two up front, probing the opposition defenders into trying to play around them and force long balls where Wendie Renard can win the aerial duel and regain possession. The 4-4-2 shape has been a long-standing out-of-possession shape used by the team, but the 2019/20 season saw a slight tactical rethink by Vasseur where he wanted to control the opposition in the central areas by using a diamond shape instead of a flat 4-4-2. The main objective was to ensure Lyon maintain horizontal compactness in these areas.

Looking at the teams in the UEFA Women's Champions League that season, a lot of them played with a line of four midfielders, which meant Lyon needed to keep their central areas from being overrun. One wide player would move into a centre-forward position, while the other would tuck into a midfield slot to ensure central compactness. The team rotates together towards the side the ball is on, prompting the interior midfielders and full-backs to press if the ball goes down the flanks. This ensures that, wherever the opposition decides to build out from, Lyon are covered. The front two will not engage in a heavy press, but rather remain close enough to make their presence felt. The hard graft is done by those farther back in midfield. If the forwards feel as though the opposition are lingering on the ball too much, they then begin to press to force the tempo. Lyon's underlying objective is to dictate the tempo of the game with and without the ball.

Figure 8 shows Lyon's shape out of possession as explained above in a league game against Paris Saint-

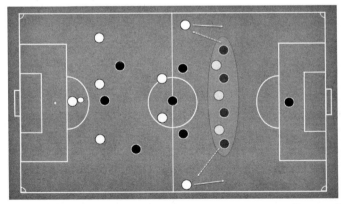

[FIGURE 8]

Germain. Notice the shorter gaps between each bank of four, where they do not want to give Paris Saint-Germain's three forwards time and space to operate in. PSG's main striker and right-sided wide forward are more central players, so in this situation they would be negated by Lyon's narrow back four. While the two Paris full-backs are free, both Lyon full-backs will be able to press the wide areas while support arrives in the form of the wingers or midfielders.

To combat the problem of leaving the wide areas too exposed, the shape is changed again. When playing passes through midfield, Lyon create superiority in midfield and defence by morphing into a type of 3-4-1-2 shape. Moving from the 4-4-2 diamond to this 3-4-1-2 is achieved by one of the full-backs pushing into a midfield position to give them better cover across the midfield area. The team don't want to be in a situation where they become overrun in any third, so they use these positional rotations to adapt and bring players where needed. While the main objective remains the same, this shape aids their pressing strategy. The 4-4-2 diamond is used to hold shape and dictate the opposition's movement, while the 3-4-1-2 allows Lyon to press intensely in midfield through their midfielders and full-backs, as is seen in *Figure 9* (opposite). Alternatively, the 3-4-1-2 shape also caters for counter-attacking and creating passing lanes, but it also allows them to utilise the pace from the full-backs to cover for Renard's lack of pace whether they move horizontally or vertically, due to the high line they hold.

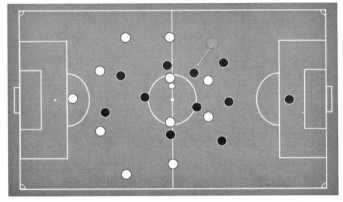

[FIGURE 9]

So far, you can see that the full-backs have an important tactical role in the side, with each one tasked with their own individual roles. By default, one full-back will play slightly higher and wider while the other tucks into a narrower position. One full-back will often play a more defensive role, acting as a third midfielder and central defender, mirroring Kyle Walker's role at Manchester City, or David Alaba's at Bayern Munich when Guardiola was in charge. From here, the full-back can drive inside to press the interior ball-carrier or move outside to pressure the opposition winger along with Lyon's winger. For the most part, Lucy Bronze plays a more tactical role because of her high footballing IQ. Though she regularly pushes up as a build-up source while in possession, she's also able to become a spare player in defensive situations.

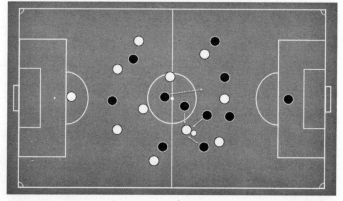

[FIGURE 10]

As *Figure 10* illustrates, Lyon are able to keep the central areas compact and shift towards the side of the ball. If it moves into the central area, then up to three players will move in to help press and close the player down. There is a constant movement with the defensive midfielder moving across to cover for the central midfielder, while the attacking midfielder drops in to cover the holding midfielder's movement. This illustration also depicts Lyon's desire for compactness and overloads in midfield and defence. If teams succeed in bypassing the press, it gives Lyon enough time to move into position to defend against crosses if it comes to it.

One of the key themes highlighted in the attacking analysis chapters is Lyon's smart use of positional rotations in the attacking system. Vasseur has used positional rotations effectively in a defensive setting to ensure there is enough cover when players move into attacking areas to prevent them from being overwhelmed. Lyon's entire structure and system is predicated on the use of positional rotations and players understanding the system inside out. To avoid repetition, this chapter will only detail the use of positional rotations in defensive situations.

So how does this integrate into Lyon's defensive strategy? The core fundamental philosophy comes down to the two defensive midfielders and full-backs. These players are critical to the way Lyon position and move across the pitch to ensure they gain superiority. Starting with the two midfielders, they position themselves in such a way that they are in parallel to each other at all times, regardless of their position. On the ball, one player will remain in a more advanced position while the other will take up a more defensive stance, allowing the latter to fill in at full-back or centre-back when either player vacates their position (in the case of the full-back moving up to press or hold a higher position). The defensive midfielders require superior positional intelligence and understanding to play the role. One example revolves around defensive awareness.

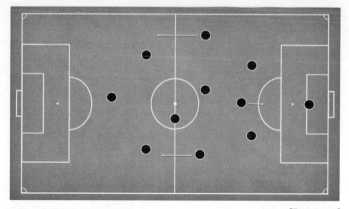

[*FIGURE 11*]

When the opposition move closer to the 18-yard box, one of the midfielders will slot in between the centre-backs to create an extra body at the back, which triggers the full-backs to push up. This is where Lyon have enough bodies in the box to withstand any counter-attacks with at least three players in the backline, as is represented in *Figure 11*. In this case, the defensive midfielder slotting in at centre-back is a signal to use another build-up strategy. At other times, the midfielders will observe and react to positions that are vacant and slot in to provide cover, whether it be at full-back or other areas in midfield. The full-backs are important in this system; shades of Pep Guardiola's influence can be seen here too in his use of inverted full-backs. The Spaniard used them to improve central control and help regain possession in these areas. Only when there are enough numbers at the back will the full-backs make their way to central midfield and press there.

Chapter 6

Pressing Structure

IN THE 2019/20 season, Lyon had the lowest rating in Passes allowed Per Defensive Action (PPDA) of the top European teams (5.10), which suggests they have an intense pressing strategy. Teams including Paris Saint-Germain, Bayern Munich, Wolfsburg, Arsenal, Chelsea, Manchester City, Atlético Madrid and Barcelona were involved in the sample, so considering who they were up against, Lyon's output in this context is impressive. Paris Saint-Germain recorded the second-lowest rating with 5.14 to give some context to their results.

There are a couple of factors that can be attributed to their position. Lyon's out-of-possession 4-4-2/4-4-2 diamond shape is the primary reason for their ability to establish a low PPDA. Holding a firm shape gives the opposition a very limited number of passing options, which forces them to play long or direct into midfield.

In the case of the diamond, teams will need to use the wide areas if they want to find a way out of traffic. In either situation, Lyon are able to quickly activate their press once possession moves into midfield, leveraging their advantage of numbers in the area. The opposition's long passes amount to 16.57 per cent when playing against Lyon, which is high given they play quick passing football. Secondly, teams that play against Lyon average 2.41 passes per possession, which means for every time they have the ball, they only make two or three passes. This suggests Lyon have a very aggressive off-the-ball style of play and do not want to give the opposition time to pass and be settled.

Now, how do the reasons discussed translate into their on-pitch decisions? Lyon's pressing strategy revolves around a midfield press. The team isn't too concerned with pressing from the front because teams will not always play out from the back, but will sometimes play a couple of passes before playing direct. The only time the forwards get involved in a high press is when the opposition wins back the ball around their own box, or if they feel the opposition is struggling to find a feasible way forward.

Their overall pressing strategy is based on trapping teams in overloads by committing two to three players to win back possession. The trigger is when it's lost in transition or when the opposition is playing through midfield during their build. When play reaches midfield, this triggers Lyon's midfield to start pressing first through the closest player, often Amandine Henry or Saki Kumagai as the first line of defence, but on occasion Dzsenifer Marozsán, Amel Majri or Lucy Bronze will be present to start the press in midfield. There are usually two to three players in the vicinity of the ball-carrier to engage in a heavily pressured pressing system. The idea is to force the opposition into a misplaced pass or win back possession through a tackle or interception. The two defensive midfielders are vital to the way Lyon operate both on and off the ball.

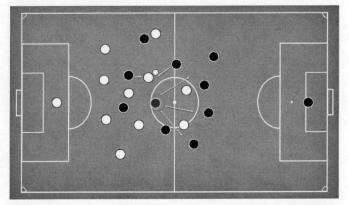

[FIGURE 12]

This is seen in practice in *Figure 12* against Montpellier who are looking to build an attack through the central areas. Note the positioning of the players in the illustration as Renard, Griedge Mbock Bathy, Kumagai and Greenwood make up a back four, with Majri, Henry, Bronze and Delphine Cascarino in midfield. Bronze cuts inside and is the first to start pressing the midfielder. The positioning of the pivot (Henry) is important in both helping the press and covering for any potential passes or runs in behind. When the ball is passed down, it prompts Majri to start pressing. The new ball-carrier manages to play a pass behind Majri which is then intercepted by Henry, who is able to protect her back line because of her expert positioning.

Lyon's defensive work has not received the same amount of plaudits so far, with much of the attention given to their electrifying attack. While it's true that they boast world-class defenders such as Renard, Bronze, Mbock and Kadeisha Buchanan, their effective and seamless integration into Vasseur's tactics has been excellent. The tactical flexibility of Bronze is a particular highlight; she is able to interchange from attacking right-back to a third central defender in a back three in a matter of seconds.

When analysing the defensive structure of any team, it's easy to focus on the defenders. However, Lyon's two central midfielders have proven to be extremely important to the overall system, and allow the team to function efficiently and effectively in both an attacking and defensive capacity. There are multiple examples of their importance through positional rotations and pressing by being in the right place to cover the possible space the ball-carrier will move into.

Their abilities to maintain such discipline and high level of concentration week in and week out for ten years has been outstanding. Given that Renard has practically been at Lyon her whole career and has led the defensive charge, it's impressive to see the tactical acumen of the players that have come in and been able to adapt. Ada Hegerberg told us about the importance of the team knowing and understanding their roles in a structure that is so fluid and it is because of this that they've been able to be extremely successful both offensively and defensively.

Chapter 7

Wendie Renard

'It was destiny.' – Wendie Renard

IN THE words of Wendie Renard, it was fate that led her to become Olympique Lyon's most successful player, and most importantly to football itself. In some ways, it seems very apt for women's football's most prestigious and successful club side in Europe. A personal read on *The Players' Tribune* describes Renard's life growing up in detail, and also gives us an insight into what made her who she is today. Reading about Renard's formative years really puts her achievements into perspective and you begin to understand what it means to come from a small town – or island in this case – to the big city, with its bright lights and unwavering allure of the high life.

Let's take this back, all the way back, to the island of Martinique in an area called Le Prêcheur where

Renard spent most of her childhood and early teenage years. The 'end of the world' is how she describes the island, where she would wake up to some gorgeous views and the warm blue waters that seemingly melted into the horizon. From kicking in her mother's belly to squabbling with siblings for the chance to watch football on the TV, football has been a significant feature in her life. The youngest of four daughters, Renard was the sports-obsessed one, with her mother regularly joining her in watching matches as she grew up. Having played a little herself, her mother understood Renard's love for the game and encouraged it. The French defender credits the women in her family for pushing her towards football, but it's her male role model that played a critical role in making her who she is as a person and player today.

Adversity is something Renard has experienced throughout her life, and one such instance is the passing of her father. He played a hugely important part in her life, and one that many daughters can relate to. He wasn't a typical father who enjoyed sports, though, but rather one who was very much into politics. Despite the two not having a major common interest to bond over, they were still very close. Renard would glue herself to her father if she could, wanting to go everywhere with him, whether it was to work or elsewhere. One day she was told the devastating news that her father had been diagnosed with lung cancer. Renard lost her father at the age of eight, and while the pain was immeasurable, the final conversation she had in the hospital room before his passing would change her life forever, and how she wanted to live it.

Her footballing career was the glitz and glamour that is seen in her star-studded journey. Her early footballing icons were Ronaldinho and Marinette Pichon, the latter of whom was the reason for her love of the French national team and the inspiration to don the iconic jersey. However, once she got to France, her role model was the Portuguese superstar Cristiano Ronaldo. She highlights two particular reasons in her account on *The Players' Tribune*, citing his 'work ethic' and 'trophies'. The winning mentality he developed throughout his career by winning accolade after accolade is something Renard wants to replicate in her career. It's also why she's been at Lyon for 13 years; despite having had the opportunity to ply her trade elsewhere, she wanted to build an unreachable legacy and be considered one of the all-time greats.

It all started on one portentous day in Martinique at the age of 14 when she received a phone call from one of her coaches about a trial at the world-famous *Clairefontaine*. She immediately flew to France for it, but upon arrival she felt inferior to the other girls, coming from a small island in the Caribbean. They were locally scouted, so how could a girl from Martinique be something special? The week passed and she eagerly awaited the results, but to her great sadness she was not selected. Renard phoned her coach and gave him the bad news, but he instructed her to wait until he made a few more phone calls. He called her back after making a call to a friend with a trial arranged at Olympique Lyon, and the rest is history – or rather more fittingly, destiny.

Renard has been an integral player as part of Lyon's defence for over a decade. A naturally gifted defender, she is an imposing figure and one that has been a reliable defensive presence since first playing for the senior team over a decade ago. Her role is that of a ball-playing centre-back where her main job is to distribute play out to the defensive midfielders and full-backs as part of their progression tactics.

Renard's abilities stretch to more than just her passing capabilities. A defensive lynchpin, her spatial and positional awareness are key parts of her excellent defensive repertoire, allowing her to identify when and where opposing attackers will be to ensure they are stopped as early as possible. Even at the other end of the pitch, she has been incredibly influential, specifically from set pieces. Her masterful aerial ability is probably Renard's strongest trait, which is evident from a career that has spanned 370 games, yielding 116 goals. This is comparable to most strikers, let alone defenders.

Renard's strengths and major attributes revolve around passing, defensive positional intelligence and aerial prowess. The French centre-back has been an immeasurable defensive powerhouse who has always played to her strengths. Lacking in pace, Renard uses her positioning as a basis of her defending. Being able to move into good defending positions early helps her to eradicate mistakes, or at the very least, she's able to delay the attacker long enough for her covering centre-back partner to arrive. At 30 years old, Renard is an experienced practitioner who has learnt to adapt her game against different opposition, which has contributed to her longevity in the side. In a system that requires proficiency on the ball, Renard has that in abundance. Not only does it mean playing passes out from the back and distributing possession, but also being able to cope under pressure in possession from opposition attackers. Renard embodies just that and is able to thrive under pressure both on and off the ball. The more experienced and higher-quality sides are more willing to attack Lyon's central defenders, which means they need to be able to deal with the press.

Probably her standout quality is her leadership, which is evident with her demeanour on the pitch and reflected in her status as club captain. Though the captain's armband is not always important for the more senior members of a dressing room, Renard's leadership involves being vocal and leading through her play. It's what keeps Lyon afloat at the back. While there have been individually brilliant defensive players throughout the years, Renard has been a pillar of solidarity and her ability to command her back four and defensive midfielders (some of whom are seasoned veterans and superstars in their own right) is impressive, to put it mildly. Knowing how to organise the back four and be constantly communicating with her defensive partners ensures everyone is always on the same page.

This is especially vital when the full-backs push forward as part of their attacking strategy. If there happens to be a turnover, then immediately being able to cover and coordinate her nearby teammates becomes critical. Renard's style of play is truly world class, with different parts of her game comparable to some exceptionally talented centre-backs. The Lyon captain's game is reminiscent of Virgil van Dijk and Sergio Ramos. These central defenders are stalwarts of Liverpool and Real Madrid respectively, with Renard equally as important for Lyon. She has the intelligent defensive positioning and command of van Dijk, as well as the attacking instincts and aggression of Ramos. These qualities make her arguably the most feared central defender in women's football.

Lyon play a high line, given they dominate possession in most, if not all, of their games. This means both Renard and her centre-back partner, either Kadeisha Buchanan or Griedge Mbock Bathy, have been the team's sweepers in the event of long balls being played over the top. She is able to predict and understand how certain attacking moves will pan out, meaning she's ready to move into position quickly. When you look at the type of opposition that come up against Lyon, it's mainly teams that want to soak up pressure and either hit them on the counter-attack or launch long balls in behind the high defensive line. Each scenario requires concentration and focus, with different skill sets needed to stop both methods of attack. Renard is excellent at using the strengths of her teammates around her while bringing her own capabilities to the fore.

This part will discuss how she's able to use her positioning effectively in both scenarios and how it makes her such a credible centre-half. When it comes to counter-attacks, Renard is theoretically most vulnerable because of the high line and her lack of pace. However, there are ways in which she's able to nullify her exposure to this. In this case, she uses the speed and work rate of Buchanan/Mbock, and the closest full-back, to move into a better covering position when it comes to counter-attacks. In doing so, Renard is able to drop deeper and position herself in a place that blocks a cross, which is ideal because of her height and dominant frame, or she is able to engage in a defensive duel in a less threatening position. Even if she isn't able to dispossess the ball-carriers, she delays them long enough for more bodies to arrive to support her.

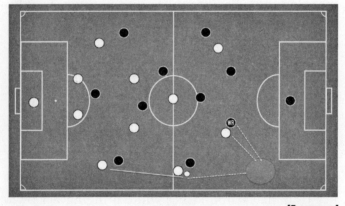

[FIGURE 13]

In *Figure 13* you can see an example of Renard's positioning when it comes to counter-attacks. Here, a long pass is made down the right flank which is aimed towards the opposition's right-winger. Renard is in a central position marking the striker, but is wary of the ball missing the intended target or left-back, and starts making a move towards the right channel. The ball misses everyone and both Renard and the striker give chase, but in this case, the centre-back is able to outmuscle the striker and deal with the situation because she had anticipated the move. This exemplifies her intelligent positioning, allowing her to easily move wider and anticipate a situation where her teammate isn't able to deal with the initial pass. While 3.31 defensive duels per 90 (76 per cent success rate) is not a very high number, you have to keep in mind that Renard is not exposed to many duels because of Lyon's possession-hungry tactics. The French defender's 76 per cent success rate is indicative of her focus on each of her duels and how she's switched on while defending against strikers.

When it comes to long balls over the top, Renard often aims to get herself under the flight of the ball and deal with it there. A lot of the time, goalkeeper Sarah Bouhaddi will sweep up behind and deal with any balls that escape both the attacker and defender. This leads us to Renard's excellence in the air. Her frame makes her an obvious target, but the 6ft 2in centre-back uses her height well as she is a threat at both ends of the pitch. In a defensive capacity, Renard is able to tower over players to clear any danger from set pieces. The statistics clearly indicate her strength in this area with 4.49 aerial duels per 90 alongside a monstrous 70 per cent success rate. The defender is one of the best in the air and is one of the reasons why Lyon have conceded so few goals, especially from set pieces. In the same UEFA Women's Champions League campaign, she ranked seventh for aerial duels (24), with five coming in her own penalty area where she registered a 100 per cent success rate. So when it comes to defending crosses or set pieces in her own 18-yard box, Renard is second to none.

When she's in the opposition box, Renard is equally strong – if not better – when it comes to attacking set pieces. The number of goals she's scored is incredible, with a record better than many attackers. On penalty duty too, Renard comes up with goals when it most matters, with strikes in UEFA Women's Champions League knockout rounds and finals. The winning goal against Paris Saint-Germain Féminine in the semi-finals of the 2019/20 season was a standout moment after toiling against a vigilant defensive performance from the Parisians.

Her movement in the opposition box during set pieces is elusive. Looking at her size, you'd think she'd be a lot slower in her movements, but Renard is able to make small bursts in the box where she loses her marker and is able to rise highest to meet an incoming cross. *Figure 14* is a representation of the goal she scored against Paris Saint-Germain and how she was able to evade her marker. Starting on the far side at the back of the queue, Renard makes a move around the defender and times her run perfectly to the front to head the ball past goalkeeper Christiane Endler.

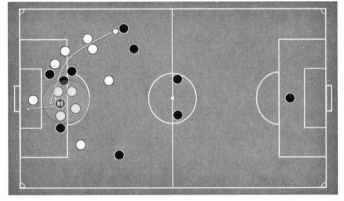

[FIGURE 14]

From a defensive perspective, Renard is defined by how sufficiently proactive she is and her excellent reading of the game, making her an all-encompassing central defender with strength, power, poise and intelligence. Over the years you've seen many slow centre-backs possess world-class qualities and dominate defences for many years. John Terry led Chelsea to numerous titles in his reign at Stamford Bridge, while Thiago Silva impressed thoroughly throughout his time with

AC Milan and, most recently, Paris Saint-Germain and Chelsea. The similarity between these two legendary defenders and Renard is their ability to lead and stand up when the team need them most. Their intelligence off the ball was always a key component of their games and was what increased the longevity of their careers.

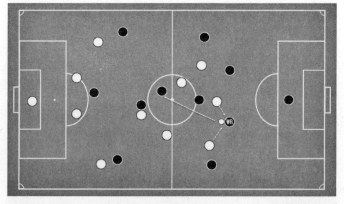

[FIGURE 15]

However, the one key difference here is that Renard's capabilities on the ball are quite good. In Lyon's fluid formation, the defenders need to have good ball-playing abilities. While the full-backs must be capable ball progressors, Renard is the initial outlet to play out from the back in build-up. Her role here is to ensure the ball is first played into the full-backs to progress it forwards – without being dispossessed – by advancing, pressing forwards. As has been mentioned, Lyon will face teams that will look to press them high, but Renard has a knack of being able to play out of the press and find a way out through her diverse range of passing, as illustrated in *Figure 15* (opposite). Here, she's comfortable in picking up possession deep and looks for short passes or longer ones in the wide areas. If teams choose to sit back and not engage in a high press, Renard will play horizontal passes between the defenders until they find an opening farther forward. Either through progressing the ball forward herself or by passing it into the central midfielders, Renard is comfortable with either option and can bypass the first line of pressure, whether it be high up the pitch or in the middle.

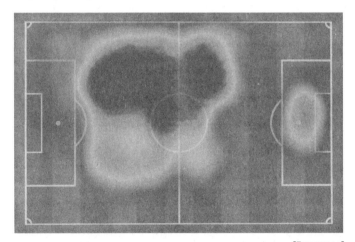

[FIGURE 16]

Figure 16 is Renard's heat map which indicates her general movement patterns and areas she most occupies. What is most surprising is how active the Lyon captain is in midfield. Part of the reason behind this is Lyon's high defensive line which naturally pushes her up the field more, but it's also because she's encouraged to step up if the opportunity presents itself. Lyon want to open as many avenues as possible in build-up which makes them unpredictable. Whether it be through the central defenders, full-backs or central midfielders, each avenue presents its own unique method of build-up.

This chapter has touched upon Renard's ability on the ball under pressure, which is both an innate quality of Renard's, but also a team requirement. Their style of play is predicated on a high level of quality ball-playing defenders, which creates the foundation of their underlying game plan. With Renard at the heart of Lyon's defence, she becomes one of the main components of their build-up and is subsequently exposed to high-pressing opposition. Though she can find her way out of pressure situations, Renard is not afraid to boot the ball into Row Z if necessary, which again speaks volumes for her intelligence as a defender. Centre-backs are often guilty of overplaying, even in pressure situations, and resisting the option to kick the ball out for a throw-in, but Renard is comfortable with this approach.

Figure 17 takes an example from a league game from the 2020/21 season against Guingamp. Renard is

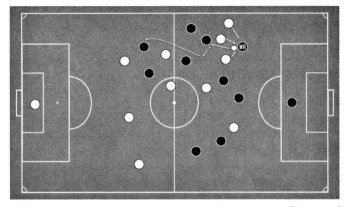

[FIGURE 17]

in a situation where possession is turned over to Lyon in their defensive half, with Guingamp actively trying to counter-press. In doing so, the centre-forward is pressing Renard and is running out of space, but she manages to exchange passes with right-back Ellie Carpenter, and find a way into the vacant space in behind. From here, she's free to play a long pass to alleviate pressure off the back line or drive forward herself. The main takeaway here is Renard's ability to work under pressure and assess the situation and promptly find a solution that works.

Renard is Lyon through and through. The captain of *Les Lyonnaises* has the red, white and blue running through her veins and has been the epitome of the unbelievable success the club have had in the last decade. Having been at the club since 2006, there are very few players in the women's game who have stayed in one place. A player's cycle is very much one to two years at most, with stays longer than three years considered long-term stints. Renard has been at the club for over a decade and is the one player who has seen the highs and lows of Lyon, and has gone through multiple iterations of teams that have been successful over the years. She's played with some big-name players such as Élodie Thomis, Hope Solo, Alex Morgan, Megan Rapinoe, Aly Wagner, Lucy Bronze and Élise Bussaglia. The experience of playing with these aforementioned players has made her a better player, but it also allowed her to be exposed to many different cultures that have shaped the way she's able to lead the team both on and off the pitch.

In an exclusive chat, Jess Fishlock, revealed that Renard was one of the players who made an effort to speak to the players, especially the foreign ones, and was one of the most charismatic characters in the dressing room. It comes as no surprise that Renard resonates with the qualities and personality the club tries to imbue: a strong winner's mentality combined with a delicate and enchanting demeanour that makes them a likeable club for neutrals to support. It was only fitting to start off our look at the players with Wendie Renard because she's the heart and soul of the club

– what better way to elaborate on Lyon's reasons for domination than to describe the captain of Olympique Lyon and first Queen of Europe?

Chapter 8

Saki Kumagai

*'I hope to keep showing what I can do
as a Japanese player at the top level.'* –
Saki Kumagai

THE JAPANESE have been known for their engineering excellence, harbouring some of the world's most innovative brands that you use on a daily basis. It's not just their sleek and futuristic designs that stand out but their quality of manufacturing. They even have a manufacturing system to increase the efficiency and efficacy of their results called kanban. It is a scheduling system for just-in-time manufacturing, and this is reflected in their people. They know their roles down to the last detail and carry out everything without a fuss.

This is what Lyon bought when they decided to move for Saki Kumagai.

Kumagai has been the underlying instrument that has given Lyon the drive they needed to run smoothly. Ever since her transfer to the French champions, Kumagai has won a title in every season. As of 2020, Kumagai has won a World Cup, seven French domestic titles, five UEFA Women's Champions Leagues and one Asian Games gold medal – quite an impressive résumé for a player who turned 30 in October 2020 and is showing no signs of slowing down. Kumagai has brought a real stability and humility to Lyon's midfield, where she's been able to do the dirty work while allowing the likes of Amandine Henry, Dzsenifer Marozsán and Eugénie Le Sommer to express themselves without worrying about what's happening behind them. Just as she's said in her quote, Kumagai has quietly been able to produce at the top level consistently for years.

Her rise in football is quite spectacular. After graduating from high school, she joined Urawa Reds in 2009 where the club won the Nadeshiko League in 2009. Her performances in Japan prompted Europe's gaze to fall on her and in July 2011, she moved to German Frauen-Bundesliga club Frankfurt. After she played two seasons for them, she made the biggest step of her career to French juggernauts Olympique Lyon in June 2013, and the rest is history.

Kumagai's role in the side is not exactly understated but can definitely be overlooked, seeing as she plays one of the least glamorous parts. However, it is the most important. Kumagai is the player that makes Lyon tick and is arguably the lynchpin that allows the team to function like a well-oiled machine.

Naturally a defensive midfielder, Kumagai is equally comfortable playing as a central defender, as she does for Japan. This trait alone makes her a valuable asset for Lyon as it gives her a better understanding of the decisions that need to be made in this position. Kumagai's main attributes revolve around her positional intelligence which contributes to her passing and defensive capabilities from a deeper position.

The Japanese international is extremely comfortable in possession, making her on-the-ball skills as impressive out of possession. Being at the base of midfield means that she's not only responsible for protecting the back four, but also plays a crucial role in build-up and relieving pressure when teams look to press Lyon high.

In 123 appearances for the club, Kumagai has had a habit of coming up with important goals, having scored 23 for the club so far.

Due to her ability to understand space from a defensive perspective, Kumagai is able to move into spaces farther forward if the opportunity presents itself.

However, more often than not her priority is to defend first, attack second.

It's imperative to understand the system she plays under at Lyon and her role in it. Kumagai plays as part of the double pivot in the 4-2-3-1 setup, with the club rarely using another formation. They rely on their superiority in possession to ensure they keep the opposition as far away from their goal as possible but use their two central midfielders like a pendulum to create balance.

Kumagai is often partnered with Amandine Henry, who is considered to be the best in her position, and the duo are the perfect foil for each other. While Henry is the more aggressive player of the two, Kumagai will position herself near her teammate to provide cover and support in both attacking and defensive situations at all times. Kumagai is responsible for the defensive assuredness of the team.

Over the course of Kumagai's time at Lyon her influence has grown from a defensive standpoint. The type of movement and sense of positioning required to play the defensive midfield position is vital, especially in Lyon's 4-2-3-1 system. Kumagai's positioning is her core strength and what keeps Lyon defensively astute. The type of opposition only determines how far forward Kumagai will be on the pitch as her role doesn't change too much. Against teams that are likely to sit deep and counter-attack, Kumagai will naturally be closer to the attackers but is more cautious against the counter-attack. Against teams that will look to press and attack Lyon a bit more, Kumagai will become the deepest-lying midfielder, acting as the primary protector with Henry supporting.

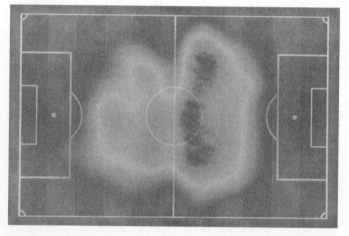

[FIGURE 18]

Taking a closer look at Kumagai's heat map in *Figure 18*, a lot of her activity is across the centre of the park. Part of the reason for her increased activity higher up is because of the high defensive line the defence holds, which naturally pushes Kumagai forward. Otherwise, there is a good amount of coverage across the third. The midfielder is an excellent reader of the game and her impeccable positioning means she knows when she can vacate her position to either attack or thwart opposition counter-attacks. This positioning gives her an ample amount of time to pick her defensive action of choice. Her composure when deciding whether she should make an interception or tackle becomes important by helping her avoid giving away needless free kicks or even giving Lyon a potential turnover.

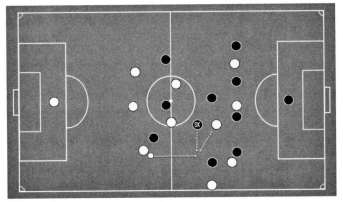

[FIGURE 19]

Take this example in *Figure 19*, where Kumagai is up against Bayern Munich in the 2019/20 UEFA Women's Champions League quarter-final. This sequence essentially portrays Kumagai's positional awareness and quick reactions to stop an opposition attack through a few simple movements. The Munich-based team are building up an attack and are looking to play down the right flank, which prompts Lyon to switch their focus to that side. While the obvious target is situated on the touchline, there is another Munich player drifting into the right channel to create an overload against Lyon's left-back and left-winger. Kumagai senses this early and steps across to intercept the second pass and gain possession back for the French side. While here she halted an attack in her own half, she is equally capable of doing the same in the opposition's defensive third.

Kumagai boasts high figures over the course of the 2019/20 season (all statistics used here will be per 90 minutes from Division 1 Féminine and the UEFA Women's Champions League). She made 12 recoveries with 69 per cent in the opposition's half, which only further solidifies our notion of the high line and her immense ability to play in one. Her 4.94 interceptions (73 per cent won) and 6.99 defensive duels (79 per cent won) show that, defensively, Kumagai is extremely busy but successful. She is also the first line of defence before opposition forwards are exposed to the back four.

Her relationship with Henry is equally as important because not only does it allow the French midfielder to play her natural game, but it enables Kumagai to press aggressively in midfield without worrying about leaving gaps behind. Henry and Kumagai play as a pendulum and provide the necessary balance to one another. When one pushes up, the other drops deep to cover.

Neither player is positioned far apart which gives them total security in midfield. It's what makes them such a devastating duo.

Figure 20 is illustrative of this, where their positioning is apparent against the Paris Saint-Germain attack. Kumagai and Henry are positioned across from each other and when the ball is played across, Kumagai presses the receiver, while Henry holds her position which gives the back four protection. Given there are no real passing options to the opposition's right side, Henry covering her side means Lyon should deal with this situation and counter.

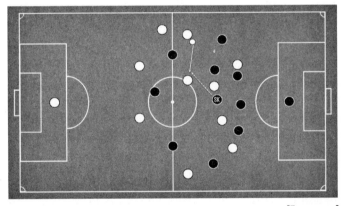

[FIGURE 20]

A lot of Lyon's Champions League success has come against stronger opposition in the later rounds, given that Lyon blew away teams in the initial stages of the tournament. This is where Kumagai shines best as these teams have the quality of players to carry out more complex tactical instructions. Teams like Wolfsburg, Bayern Munich, Paris Saint-Germain and Arsenal play an aggressive game and are more willing to go toe to toe with Lyon than weaker opponents are. This was seen throughout last season's tournament, and there were times the team struggled, but one constant remained: Kumagai.

They conceded two goals from the quarter-finals to the final – against Bayern Munich, Paris Saint-Germain and Wolfsburg – and in all three ties, they were on the back foot for a period of time. Kumagai's intelligent positioning, her quick closing down of ball-carriers and smart interceptions shut down attacks before they could pose a major threat. Her discipline in front of the back four was a constant factor which led to their impressive backs-against-the-wall performances.

Kumagai's off-the-ball movement and positioning also has an influence on the way Lyon attack and build up play. The defensive midfielder will either drop in to become a third centre-back when the other two split wide or she'll stay in her midfield position. When she becomes a third central defender, the full-backs are given more licence to push forward as Kumagai offers the backline insurance alongside the ever-present central midfielder who will move into the vacant full-back position. When she stays in midfield, the full-backs will invert and come inside to protect the half-spaces with the wingers pushing high wide. In both scenarios, it is Kumagai's movement that determines how Lyon will attack. This was especially evident in the 2019/20 UEFA Women's Champions League campaign.

Lyon arguably have some of the finest defenders in women's football, and in Renard an excellent centre-back. However, her lack of pace is an issue. Kumagai ensures Renard is not exposed to quick attackers and stops them from going into space behind the high line. From what has been detailed above, it is conclusive that Kumagai's defensive and off-the-ball role is critical to the team's overall success.

There is a feeling that Kumagai's on-the-ball influence might not be as important as her work off it. However, the Japanese captain needs to be as excellent on the ball as she is off it to comply with the overall tactical philosophy of the team. Lyon play with a high defensive line and, while Kumagai's primary responsibility is to shield and protect the back four, it is not uncommon to see Kumagai make forays forward to provide the more attacking players with a recyclable passing option or play penetrative passes from deep. There are periods where Lyon will apply lots of pressure tp opposition defences, pushing them back for long periods, which means the team will naturally push higher.

What this does mean is that, while Kumagai's primary job is to stop any potential counter-attacks if Lyon give up possession, she is also the player who will play simple passes to keep possession in Lyon's hands. With the two quickest defenders being the full-backs who are thus positioned slightly higher, it makes Kumagai's positioning and awareness that much more important, meaning balance between attack and defence is key. It is this positioning that also allows Kumagai to efficiently play passes from her midfield position. Kumagai has two functions when it comes to the transitional phase, the first of which is to aid in build-up and the second is to be a recycling passer farther up the pitch.

Lyon's build-up structure, in a nutshell, is to invite pressure in order to create spaces in between the lines. Goalkeeper Bouhaddi will often look to find one of the centre-backs or defensive midfielders who are close to the box, especially when the opposition are committing numbers high. The full-backs will push up slightly while the number ten will drop into central midfield to become another passing option. Kumagai is excellent under pressure, which means giving her possession in tight spaces allows this plan to work. Play from the back goes through Kumagai or Henry, whether it's through the first or second pass. When Kumagai is in possession, she will look towards finding her defensive midfield partner or one of the full-backs, even if it means playing a series of lateral or horizontal passes which will eventually open up small gaps to progress play forward.

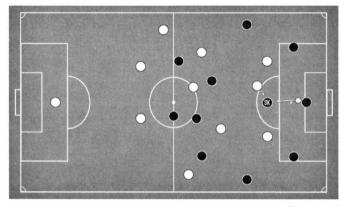

[FIGURE 21]

Taking a closer look at Lyon's build-up against a high-pressing team, *Figure 21* is a representation of a passage of play against Paris Saint-Germain in the 2019/20 UEFA Women's Champions League semi-final. Here you can see the Parisian club match Lyon in a three v three situation which has created space in behind. Kumagai is positioned centrally in front of the goalkeeper. Marozsán drops into vacant space and looks to receive a pass from Bouhaddi. Now that the ball has left the box, Kumagai can push up and receive a return pass from Marozsán, and though she has pressure from the nearby centre-forward, she releases a first-time pass into Majri who is farther forward. This passage of play highlights how Lyon are able to withstand pressure from the opposition and Kumagai's importance in build-up.

In another scenario where Kumagai does drop in to become a third central defender, the full-backs are given licence to push forward more, meaning that she will naturally look for the two wide players with long-range passes if the situation allows it. Otherwise, she will opt to keep it simple and find her closest midfield teammate. The team has two world-class progressive passers in Henry and Marozsán, but both players prefer to play higher up. Although they do tend to drop deep, their primary function is to find more creative ways to get the ball to the forward players.

Kumagai's passing, from an attacking perspective, is another trait that goes under the radar because of her primary responsibilities. Kumagai is such an intelligent defender and even more exquisite when it comes to her tactical acumen. As for ball progression, we know Henry and Marozsán are key creators, but Kumagai can hold her own in this department. Due to her deep midfield position, Kumagai is able to scan the pitch and find any potential openings farther up, especially when Lyon have an opportunity to counter-attack. She doesn't rely on vision or creativity through penetrative or key passes, but rather opts for longer passes to bypass any incoming players and take advantage of the speed Lyon possess, especially in the wide areas.

From a statistical standpoint, Kumagai averaged 4.73 long passes per 90 minutes with a 64.2 per cent success rate. For a player playing so deep, a success rate of 64 per cent is astronomical given the likelihood of the ball being intercepted. Alongside this, Kumagai averaged 11.15 passes to the final third with a 79.1 per cent success rate. These are two standout statistics given Kumagai's role, but ones that show her playmaking abilities for Lyon. Compare this to Henry's 13.88 passes to the final third, and it becomes clear her influence in this regard shouldn't be overlooked. The advantage of having Kumagai play these long passes is her ability to

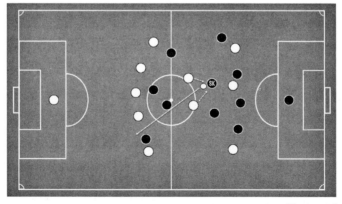

[FIGURE 22]

find players in space to latch on to them. An example of this is illustrated in *Figure 22* (on page 91) where Kumagai's long-range passing helped to create a goalscoring opportunity.

This passage of play was taken from a domestic Division 1 Féminine match against Paris Saint-Germain in the 2019/20 season where Kumagai has intercepted a through ball which has caught the Parisian club out. With the Paris Saint-Germain defensive line so high up, there are two Lyon players sitting on the shoulder of the defence. Le Sommer's position ahead of left-back Ashley Lawrence means that Kumagai sends an enticing long pass into Le Sommer's path, putting her through on goal. These kinds of passes are what Kumagai is capable of producing at any given moment. Her mind is constantly working at finding teammates and gaps in the opposition's defence.

Kumagai is a silent operator, a player who gets her job done with minimal fuss. The club is predicated on buying and developing the best players in the world. Players dream of a move to the French giants but not every international import has worked out. Global superstars such as Alex Morgan and Megan Rapinoe came in for a season and moved back. Kumagai's stint has been nothing short of remarkable and has been a beacon of stability and dependability in a side that has seen changes all around. A manager's dream, Kumagai is Lyon's engine that makes this Rolls-Royce of a team run smoothly.

Chapter 9

Eugénie Le Sommer

'For me, Eugénie Le Sommer is one of the most undervalued players in women's football.' – Jess Fishlock

A RECORD goalscorer and icon in women's football, Eugénie Le Sommer has been an integral part of French footballing history. Adored by fans and peers alike, the striker has been an ever-present figure in many France and Olympique Lyon teams over the years. Her journey into football was almost expected considering how her family was deeply connected with the beautiful game. The fifth child of nine children, Le Sommer grew up with enough to form a couple of five-a-side teams with a referee if you include her parents. Her mother, Claudine, played professionally and her father, Thierry, was a policeman, while her siblings grew up playing football too.

This sporting culture in the Le Sommer household meant her chances of playing at a professional level were significantly high from a young age. Having kicked a ball from the age of two, Le Sommer showcased a raw talent from the offset and, like many other female footballers, had to play in the boys' team in order to continue her development until her mid-teens. Though there was some reluctance from her mother to go down this pathway, she eventually agreed. Claudine Le Sommer had experienced hardship during her playing days, with women's football in the 80s having been much less respected and recognised than it is today. So it came as a surprise when her daughter asked to play for an academy at the age of four.

Le Sommer joined AS Guermeur in 1998 and exploded into life, with former coach Robert Muscat likening her to a moth because of her ability to just be everywhere. FC Lorient started an Under-15s women's team which was timely because, at 14, Le Sommer had to leave Guermeur due to the restrictions of playing in a boys' team at that age.

The move to FC Lorient where she earned many honours for the academy was the platform that propelled her career, helping them win the *Coupe Fédérale 16 ans* in 2005 and the *Mozaïc Foot Challenge* in 2006. It was this tournament that earned her a call-up to CNFE Clairefontaine where she then caught the eye of Division 1 Féminine side Stade Briochin. Her goalscoring exploits continued as she hit the back of the net ten times in her first seven league matches, which included a hat-trick against Toulouse in a 4-5 defeat. She finished the season as the league's top scorer and was awarded the UNFP Female Player of the Year the following season.

This is where Olympique Lyon started to take notice and investigate a possible move for the young centre-forward. In 2010, she made the move across to Olympique Lyon and the rest, as they say, is history. Ten years later, Le Sommer has 18 domestic and seven UEFA Women's Champions League titles. Even on an individual level, Le Sommer has been recognised at both domestic and international level, including wins of the UNFP Player of the Year twice and the France National Championship Best Striker three times. This sort of consistency and level of success is only available to a special talent.

> *'She is one of the best players at Lyon, full stop. She*
> *should be in the conversation for the Ballon d'Or.*
> *How she isn't in the top three of that blows my mind.'*
> – Jess Fishlock

Eugénie Le Sommer, Sarah Bouhaddi and Wendie Renard celebrating Lyon's seventh UEFA Women's Champions League title win in August 2020.

Manchester City Women v Olympique Lyon Féminin – UEFA Women's Champions League 2018.

Wendie Renard

Ada Hegerberg posing alongside Luka Modrić and Kylian Mbappé with her Ballon d'Or award.

The man behind the success of Olympique Lyon Féminin, Jean-Michel Aulas.

Lucy Bronze and Amandine Henry. Two stalwarts of Lyon who have been crucial to their success.

Ada Hegerberg celebrating her goal against Barcelona in the 2018 UEFA Women's Champions League Final.

Jean-Michel Aulas congratulating the team as they come to collect their medals after their seventh UEFA Women's Champions League win.

Amel Majri takes on Dominique Janssen in the last encounter between VfL Wolfsburg and Olympique Lyon Féminin.

Dzsenifer Marozsán looks to the heavens as she walks past the UEFA Women's Champions League trophy.

While many will look at Ada Hegerberg and Wendie Renard as the standout personalities and remember other superstars such as Alex Morgan when thinking of Olympique Lyon, Le Sommer deserves to be recognised as one of the very best. One of the most telling things about Le Sommer's talent is the admiration she has from her peers. During my sit-down chat with Jess Fishlock, she constantly referenced and praised the striker for her consistency, professionalism and sheer ability. For now, though, let's look at the qualities she possesses on the pitch and how she's used them to help the team.

Le Sommer is a versatile forward capable of playing in any of the front four positions. Having played as a centre-forward for the majority of her career, she is usually deployed on the left of a front three or four for Olympique Lyon. Her role is that of an advanced inside-forward who predicates herself on her excellent shot taking, dribbling and pure goalscoring ability. A very technically sound player, Le Sommer is someone who can turn games and combines well with other players around her to create goalscoring opportunities. She is the quintessential left-sided forward for a marauding full-back, who will be given licence to overlap and not only provide crosses but also to open space for Le Sommer to cut inside.

Once on the ball, she combines technique and dribbling with acceleration and good decision-making to get past her opponent and then either take a crack at goal or look for a pass. She provides a direct threat and attacking thrust alongside Olympique Lyon's other attackers. If you look at the usual suspects that line up for the team, Ada Hegerberg is the central striker and main goalscorer, Delphine Cascarino provides width, speed and crossing from the right side, and Dzsenifer Marozsán is the creative hub that looks to glue them all together.

Being a major part of Olympique Lyon's attacking moves, Le Sommer is often an outlet rather than a facilitator. Her traits are very similar to most forwards, but what sets her apart is her clinical finishing and ability to make something out of nothing. Despite being an attacking player, Le Sommer does track back, showing her willingness to be a team player, although it isn't her strongest attribute. She still provides a presence and helps out, but she's much more effective in the final third. She isn't as involved in build-up play and is one of the few players allowed to linger in the final third and be ever-present in creating chances. Having said that, Le Sommer is extremely effective at finding spaces in the box when it comes to getting on the end of crosses coming from the right-hand side. When a player like

Cascarino or Bronze accelerates and crosses, it's usually with pinpoint accuracy into dangerous areas for the likes of Le Sommer and Hegerberg to attack.

Finding a player to compare her to is not difficult because her playing style is reminiscent of a number of people, but what makes her stand out is the quality she exudes on the pitch. Her tactical intelligence, precision and pure goalscoring ability are what makes her such an elite forward. Though not a replica, Le Sommer has shades of Neymar in her game with the way she's able to effortlessly glide past players and show a sudden burst of speed to get either side of them and then get a shot away. She can turn a game on its head on her own. While not as flashy off the pitch, the comparison to the Brazilian on it is apt.

Le Sommer starts off on the left wing where she can be seen interchanging positions regularly with the central striker or attacking midfielder. The fluidity in their system and the flexibility of their attacking players to play comfortably in different positions benefit them greatly. During the 2019/20 season, we saw this in action a lot more with Hegerberg's injury. Towards the latter stages of the UEFA Women's Champions League, Le Sommer was used as a centre-forward but regularly moved around to provide her presence in other positions. Her responsibilities on the ball have been outlined extensively, while off the ball she looks to take up good attacking positions, either on the shoulder of defensive lines or in pockets of space in midfield, to pick up possession and drive. She has this ability to give space to others both on and off the ball; defenders are wary of her movement, and if she does get on the ball, she can contribute even if it's from distance.

There's no better place to start than taking a closer look at her on-the-ball skills. Le Sommer, as has been outlined, is an excellent ball-carrier. The inside-forward role is one that requires excellent dribbling, positional awareness and combination play, all of which she has in abundance. Usually in the left half-space between left wing and attacking midfield, Le Sommer wants to pick up possession in between the lines rather than hug the touchline. Though being wide isn't exactly an issue for her, she has more acceleration than pure speed. One of the reasons for this is to take advantage of her ability to create chances through her excellent dribbling and shooting abilities. The idea is to use sudden movements to find enough space to shoot. In this instance, she manages to find just enough room to get a shot away on goal. *Figure 24* on page 102 is an example that illustrates a combination of her speed, acceleration, intelligence and ability to work in small spaces. Most top attackers – especially creative, attacking dribblers – don't need much room to manoeuvre. Le Sommer falls into that category and is so proficient on the ball that even with multiple markers, she can get a shot away with a couple of yards of space.

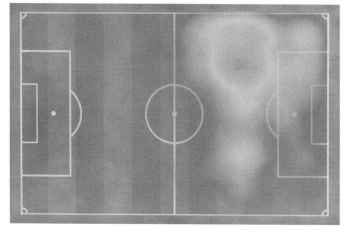

[FIGURE 23]

Figure 23 is a heat map that shows how Le Sommer's position in matches doesn't stray too far away from the half-space. Most of her activity and 'heat' is in this area, and what is most striking is the lack of activity in the penalty area. Rather than being inactive in the box, she simply doesn't spend too much time there. It's mostly Le Sommer making quick movements in one v one positions and getting her shots away or making late runs to score. Though she takes plenty of penalty-area touches – her statistics are high (7.04 per 90) – she isn't one to linger in the box; she's more likely to pick up possession outside the box and take a shot if she can. Watching her over 90 minutes, you won't see her play at a high tempo throughout, but when she does get on the ball, Le Sommer can make things happen. She plays in bursts in the final third, which allows her to overpower opposition defenders and work in small spaces if needed.

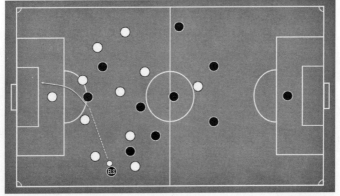

[FIGURE 24]

In *Figure 24*, taken from a match against Bordeaux, Le Sommer picks up possession wide on the left after a series of passes between herself, Majri and Selma Bacha. There is space for Le Sommer to drive into, but she is being tracked by two opposition players. She manages to drive through and take a shot from outside the 18-yard box.

Her dribble from the touchline to the box took no time at all and the ball seemed stuck to her foot. A quick shot before anyone could close her down resulted in a goal.

Her statistics reflect what she does on the pitch. During the 2019/20 season (domestic league and UWCL), Le Sommer averaged 4.01 shots (41.9 per cent on target) and 5.4 dribbles per 90 minutes (62.1 per cent successful), which indicates her high frequency of dribbles and resulting shots. Having a 60 per cent+ dribble success rate means she's able to get past players more often and move into goalscoring positions to take shots. Though her success rate is less than 50 per cent, the sheer volume means she's able to get enough shots away to trouble the goalkeeper more often than not.

An injury-hit 2019/20 season still yielded nine goals and three assists (in 966 minutes), so a fully fit Le Sommer in 2020/21 will be much more productive. She has always come up with important goals and has a knack of being in the right place at the right time. Bringing expected goals (xG) into the conversation, Le Sommer overperformed throughout the season with 0.84 goals per 90 minutes from 0.57 xG. Her movement is impeccable and will be explained in more detail a little bit later, but is one of the major reasons for her goalscoring exploits.

Building on her tactical intelligence on the ball, Le Sommer is very smart at being able to understand player positions on the pitch. Whether it's her full-back making overlapping runs or the centre-forward/right-winger making diagonal runs from the opposite side, Le Sommer makes intelligent decisions thanks to her positional awareness. Not only does being in the half-space enable her to find spaces to pick up and drive forward, but it also allows the left-back room to make an overlapping run and present a passing option.

Le Sommer is a player that has formed excellent partnerships with her full-backs because of the natural spaces the two run into. The full-back will usually want to stay wide and attack while Le Sommer wants to stay narrow. Being able to interchange seamlessly, as she's done with Amel Majri for France on multiple occasions, makes her such a dangerous proposition. The opposition have to be switched on because she either cuts inside and shoots with precision, or has created space for a marauding left-back to overlap and cross. The 2019 Women's World Cup is a prime example of the Majri/Le Sommer partnership, which time after time gave France an attacking threat down the left flank.

Picking up the ball in the position shown in *Figure 25* (opposite) is where she's normally found during Olympique Lyon's build-up. Assuming the opposition are approaching the game to sit in a medium to low block, Le Sommer will be marked by at least two players,

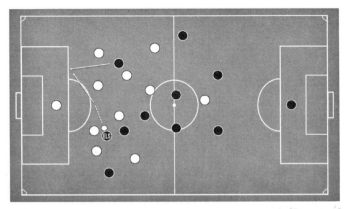

[FIGURE 25]

usually the full-back and defensive midfielder. Once she moves closer to the box, the centre-back may move across to assist. However, Le Sommer is intelligent enough to know that if a passing option is available, she should take it. When she picks up the ball here, she looks to cut inside. Her left-back is free and that momentarily takes the opposition full-back's attention away. Le Sommer will attempt to drive forward and cut inside on to her favoured right foot, where she wants to shoot. At this point, she'll be met with multiple defenders closing her down, and instead of shooting from this position, Le Sommer sees the onrushing Cascarino on the far side and threads a ball through a sea of players surrounding her. Here, she had two options: one earlier in the move to pass to the left-back, or a through ball to the right-winger's late run later on, which she took. This was possibly the better choice because there's less time for the opposition to reorganise themselves; thus, a better goalscoring opportunity is born.

Le Sommer's ball-playing skills have been well documented, but it's her off-the-ball work that makes her a quintessential Olympique Lyon player. They are very much a system-based side, which means they operate and rely on players understanding their roles both on and off the ball.

Le Sommer is one that is able to do that diligently. Someone of her calibre would usually be seen as the luxury star player that would be afforded a little extra leeway to be more static, but Le Sommer is a willing and able runner off the ball. Considering the fluidity of Olympique Lyon's frontline players, Le Sommer is best suited to this type of football because of her versatility and comfort playing as a centre-forward and left inside-forward. Being able to interchange positions at will allows other players around her to do the same and simultaneously confuses the opposing defenders. A lot of what's already been said has covered Le Sommer's general positioning in the left half-space, but what makes her such an incredible goalscorer is this movement and interchangeability. Being able to get into goalscoring positions without the ball requires a smart and intelligent mind.

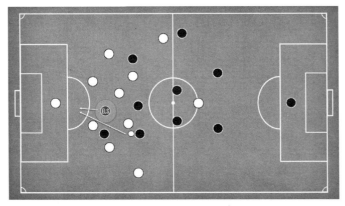

[FIGURE 26]

Playing between the lines against teams that sit back and defend requires much more intricate and smart movement because of the small spaces available. It takes precise passing and perfectly timed moves to be able to penetrate these tight defences. Olympique Lyon often face this type of opposition and all their forwards have to be proficient at breaking through. Though there are some, such as Cascarino, who thrive better in space or on the counter-attack, the likes of Le Sommer and Hegerberg can operate in tighter spaces due to their technical ability. *Figure 26* is a representation of Le Sommer's ability to ghost between the lines and end up getting in the box to latch on to a through ball or cross almost unmarked. You can see how compact the central players are, with the ball-carrier looking for options. Le Sommer's first instinct is to go forward, and she sees a gap between the central defenders which is also picked up by the ball-carrier. The incisive pass is inch-perfect and leads to Le Sommer being through on goal.

To further demonstrate Le Sommer's pure goal-scoring talent, the table below will compare the French forward against four different goalscorers and their goalscoring records from 2016 to 2019/20. The list includes some incredible wingers who have all been essential components of their teams' success over the years. Le Sommer's record against these players since 2016 speaks for itself.

Player	League Goals (2016–2019/20)
E. Le Sommer	66
G. Reiten	65
L. Martens	54
N. Parris	33
K. Diani	30
C. Hansen	29
B. Mead	25

[FIGURE 27]

The table in *Figure 27* shows exactly the kind of goalscoring form Le Sommer has been in for Olympique Lyon in recent seasons. Though she has a plethora of goals that stretch back to the 2010/11 season when she moved from Stade Briochin, Le Sommer has shown an incredible consistency against some of the biggest names in world football. Only Guro Reiten of Chelsea comes close, which speaks volumes for the kind of output the French forward has been able to produce.

At 32 years of age, Le Sommer still has a few more productive years left at the top, and while she has spoken of her desire to possibly take up a new challenge, Olympique Lyon will only benefit from her staying. Possibly a change in position will be needed as her speed starts to dwindle, but what is evidently clear is how pivotal Le Sommer has been in helping Olympique Lyon achieve a record-breaking number of UEFA Women's Champions League and Division 1 Féminine titles, not only in terms of her goals, but her leadership and 'big-game' influence too. Time and time again, Le Sommer has delivered on the biggest stage, including numerous Champions League finals and knockout stages.

The 2019/20 final against Wolfsburg saw Le Sommer open the scoring after a spell of dominance. While Hegerberg has broken records and taken the headlines since she exploded on to the scene, Le Sommer has gone about her business and helped contribute in the way she knows best – scoring goals. It's worth remembering that Le Sommer racked up 74 goals from 2010 to 2014, which is when Hegerberg arrived. Olympique Lyon's dominant reign can really be accredited to the excellent work put in by Eugénie Le Sommer, and they will have a hard time replacing her once she decides to hang up her boots in a few years' time. She's been the face of French football for the past ten years and has won everything except for a major international trophy. There is a feeling that Le Sommer is one of the greatest ever players not to have won a title for France, but for Olympique Lyon she's been a fundamental part of their sustained success in the last decade. It will be a while until another Eugénie Le Sommer appears on the scene – a generational talent.

Chapter 10

Dzsenifer Marozsán

'Dzsenifer Marozsán is your favourite player's favourite player. Her technical mastery and vision of the game are on another level.' – Arianna Scavetti

THERE ARE a few players that come along and set the world alight. There are even fewer that are generational talents with such raw potential that they're able to play the game at a different level from everyone around them. They play in slow motion where they think and see three moves ahead, making every pass and shot seem effortless. The likes of Lionel Messi, Cristiano Ronaldo, Kylian Mbappé and Neymar Jr are a few examples in the men's game where extreme potential has been realised.

Dzsenifer Marozsán is one such player in the women's game. The German international has long been touted as one of the world's best, and came close to winning the coveted Ballon d'Or Féminin in 2018 when she was placed third behind Pernille Harder (then of Wolfsburg) and teammate Ada Hegerberg. Her rise in football has been incredible – but not without hardship.

At a young age, the Budapest-born Marozsán moved to Germany where she was discovered, signing for FC Saarbrücken at the age of 14. Once her talent became apparent to the masses, the Deutcher Fussball-Bund convinced her to switch her loyalties to Germany, which she ultimately accepted, as well as naturalising her family too. At 15, she became the youngest player to appear and score in the Frauen-Bundesliga.

FC Saarbrücken were convinced by her potential early on and had no qualms in giving her game time at such a young age. In 2009, Marozsán signed for Frankfurt, who were challenging for domestic and European honours. Her seven years at the club yielded a UEFA Women's Champions League (UWCL) crown in the 2014/15 season, where she ended up as the top assister with eight and was named in the team of the tournament. In 2012, she faced Lyon for the first time in the UWCL Final, putting the French giants on the receiving end of her talents.

It was finally in 2016 that Lyon made the move to sign Marozsán and make her a core part of the first-team squad, and that's where her love affair with France and Lyon began. Marozsán has won 21 trophies in her career thus far, most notably five UWCL titles – initially with Frankfurt, and on four subsequent occasions with Lyon. Marozsán brings a winning mentality and a never-say-die attitude that stems from overcoming a serious lung illness in 2018. Marozsán suffered from a pulmonary embolism which threatened to derail her career permanently, but because of her resilience she was only out for a period of three months. Regularly touted by her peers as one the world's best players, Marozsán continues to mesmerise with her story and, most importantly, her football.

Marozsán's role for Lyon does not have an exact name but rather it consists of a mixture of past and present trends. The base role Marozsán plays is that of a classic number ten where she is deployed in central midfield alongside Amandine Henry and Saki Kumagai; however, she plays most often behind the central striker, providing a creative outlet but also making off-the-ball runs. The Lyon system is very fluid as has been mentioned, which puts the German in the bracket of the new number eight/ten hybrid player, but one that has evolved from being just a specialist number ten. You could say her qualities are very similar to what one could call a shadow striker, but with more creativity and responsibility in recycling possession in the final third.

By definition, a shadow striker operates as the team's main goalscoring threat. The shadow striker aggressively pushes forward into goalscoring positions as the ball moves into the final third and looks to close down opposing defenders when out of possession. What makes Marozsán different is the work she does off the ball as much as on it, and what the team demands of her.

Being the team's primary creative playmaker means Marozsán is responsible for creating opportunities from the attacking midfield area. She is the player that the attacking moves run through when possession moves up from midfield into the final third. Usually, she'll receive possession from one of the defensive midfielders or full-backs and look to create an attacking move with other more mobile players around her.

Simultaneously, Marozsán drops into pockets of space both in attacking and defensive areas to provide her team with a passing option during build-up and a route out of highly pressurised situations. The German is the team's core creative catalyst, while also being able to withstand pressure and contribute to the side's defensive work when it comes to pressing high up the pitch or even in the defensive third. Marozsán's shadow striker tag originates from her excellent movement both on and off the ball, which makes her an excellent forward who can score goals as well as create. Her 26 goals and 27 assists since joining the club are a testament to her all-round ability as a complete attacking midfielder.

There are no clear comparisons to make to Marozsán as her style of play is truly one of a kind in the women's game. There are shades of Marek Hamšík and Donny van de Beek who aren't exactly forwards but are more than just attacking midfielders. The German playmaker is undoubtedly someone who can turn a game on its head and provide a source of inspiration when Lyon need it. Even if she doesn't always contribute directly with goals and assists each game, her presence on the pitch creates opportunities for the players around her.

It is one of the roles in the team that possesses almost complete freedom, which allows Marozsán to have more of an influence on proceedings and shape the game to her style of play. This role played by the German international requires vision, creativity and understanding of space, which fuels her immense range of passing, dribbling and ability to make the right decisions. As has been said, Marozsán plays as part of the midfield three but moves more into an orthodox number ten role in Lyon's fluid 4-3-3 system. Her responsibilities are split into what she does on the ball and off the ball. This chapter will start off by explaining her in-possession attributes followed by her out-of-possession ones.

Arguably, Marozsán's on-the-ball ability is what sets her apart from other attacking midfielders. She sits in midfield alongside Amandine Henry and Saki Kumagai who are the primary facilitators in Lyon's build-up routine. There are two ways in which Marozsán contributes to the initial phase. Firstly, she'll always make herself available as a passing option, either for the centre-backs directly in the second line of midfield or deeper in the defensive third. Depending on the situation and opposition setup, in build-up Marozsán will adjust her position accordingly. A lot of teams choose to not only press the centre-backs and close the lanes towards the full-backs, but also to condense the spaces the defensive midfielders would usually occupy. To counteract this, Marozsán will come in to receive a lofted pass from the centre-backs and quickly turn to progress play. This not only negates the opposition's press but also allows Lyon to quickly apply pressure back on to their opponents.

Taking a look at *Figure 28*, this situation is one that Lyon and Marozsán faced last year against teams that pressed them high. Similar to the example seen in the Kumagai chapter, Lyon are in a three v three situation against Paris Saint-Germain which has created space between defence and midfield. Marozsán drops into

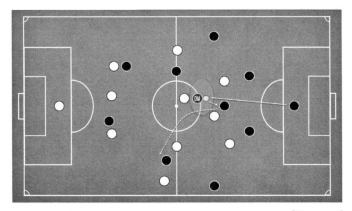

[FIGURE 28]

vacant space and looks to receive a pass from goalkeeper Sarah Bouhaddi since Kumagai is marked tightly, while the ball into the wide centre-backs could result in a loss of possession in a dangerous area. Now that the ball has vacated the box into Marozsán, Kumagai can push up and receive a return pass from the German. Though Marozsán comes under pressure from multiple players, her ability to withstand pressure and release the ball quickly is immense. The ball she releases into Kumagai is met with a first-time pass into Majri, which relieves pressure on Lyon's defence and bypasses Paris Saint-Germain's press.

Now that Marozsán's role in build-up is better understood, I will move on to explain how her strengths are utilised in the next phase. Once possession reaches the middle and final thirds, Marozsán's influence becomes much more apparent. When the German playmaker is given possession in these areas, she quickly scans the field to look for potential openings up front. Here, she decides whether to find a pass or drive herself into the final third.

Taking up either decision is based on the spaces created by the team during the build-up phase. If they've opted for a wide approach, then Marozsán possibly looks to link play and find a penetrative pass for the winger. On the other hand, if they have decided to play centrally, Marozsán would look to drive forward instead. Each decision is dependent on the opposition setup and positions at the time of receiving the pass. Whether it's a short, simple pass to the nearest player or a long pass into the channels, Marozsán's ability to combine movement and passing is unprecedented at Lyon.

Marozsán's movement is not confined to one area or space and the heat map shown in *Figure 29* is indicative

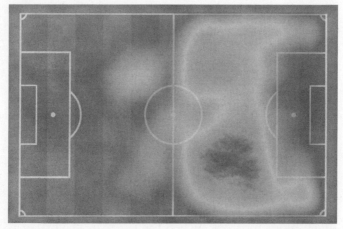

[FIGURE 29]

of this. The 'hotter' areas, so to speak, are mainly in the half-spaces, which tells us that Marozsán is a player that wants to be playing between the lines and not be predictable. This falls in line with the description of the player earlier in the chapter. Marozsán moves all across the pitch and is always looking to receive possession because she has runners ahead of her.

Statistically speaking, Marozsán is pretty proficient when it comes to her passing numbers. In the 2019/20 domestic season, she averaged 5.65 long passes (63.8 per cent completion rate), 10.17 final-third passes (70.4 per cent completion rate) and 6.35 passes to the penalty area (56.8 per cent completion rate), all per 90 minutes. She ranked second for deep completed passes per 90 minutes (a non-cross pass that is aimed for the zone within 20 metres of the opposition goal, according to Wyscout) and highest for assists with 12.

What is most prevalent about all these stats is the high volume she outputs along with very high accuracy rates and her ability to play dangerous passes close to the opposition's goal. It's one thing to have a high frequency of passes, but if they aren't accurate then they bring no value to the team. So everything needs to be put into context. What's important to take away from this data, however, is her ability to affect the attacking phase through her passing and create more goalscoring opportunities.

Marozsán's passing ability comes to the fore during quick exchanges where she passes when put under pressure. Often, when in possession near the 18-yard box, teams will look to close the space between Marozsán and goal, which means she needs to act quickly and move possession on before being dispossessed. This can be seen through her volume and accuracy of passes to the penalty area in conjunction with her heat map, which shows that most of her work comes closer to the box.

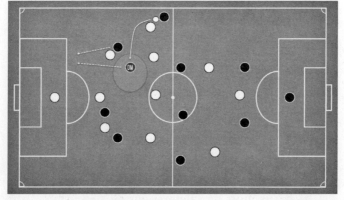

[FIGURE 30]

An example of the above point can be seen in *Figure 30* where Marozsán is in space between three opposing players with the ball situated in the wide areas. The pass from the wide player will come into Marozsán, who knows where other players are currently positioned. Once received, the next pass will be immediate and be played into her teammate making a run on the shoulder of the last defender. This sort of quick thinking and ability to get the ball out of tight areas is what makes Marozsán such a dangerous attacking midfielder.

A lot of the movements discussed have shown that Marozsán is not static, and being able to drift into different attacking areas is a vital part of her game as well as the team's tactics. Her long passing is mainly used as a line-breaking option to switch play from one flank to another when teams are compact and Lyon need to break down a resolute defensive line. Alternatively, it is used to counter-attack and progress the ball quickly and ensure that Lyon move from back to front in fewer passes to make the most of the situation.

Figure 31 is an illustration of how her long passing ability aids Lyon in breaking down opposition defences. In this situation, the opposing players are heavily positioned on the near side, and although there

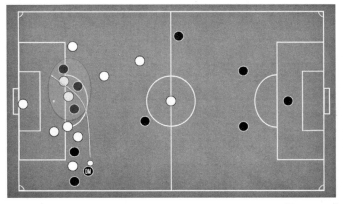

[FIGURE 31]

aren't any immediate markers or pressers, Marozsán will need to quickly switch the ball to the opposite side. In doing so, this should enable Lyon to activate the potential three v two scenario on the far side and have a better goalscoring chance against a compact defensive line.

Marozsán is a deceptively slow character on the pitch. When she's on the ball you get the sense that the opposition can dispossess her easily or that she will be unable to move from point A to point B without any trouble. However, one of Marozsán's core strengths is her ability to carry the ball effortlessly and distribute the ball to create attacking chances. As the number ten, Marozsán's ability to keep possession and move into either area to shoot or pass, as described earlier, is important.

This is the other side of her game which has helped her produce a number of goals and create clear-cut goalscoring chances throughout her career. She doesn't have the pace of more agile attacking midfielders, but what sets her apart is her ability to keep and distribute possession, or find space to take shots. This is another method of creating space by pulling in players.

Though she doesn't use dribbling as much to push forward it's important to emphasise that her ball carrying and keeping attributes are key weapons in her arsenal. In Division 1 Féminine, Marozsán averaged 2.48 dribbles per 90 minutes in the 2019/20 season, which isn't the highest. Her success rate of 60.9 per cent, however, is what makes her dribbling all the more effective, as she usually picks her moments correctly. Couple this with Marozsán's 2.91 shots per 90 minutes with 53.7 per cent of them on target, and you can see how while in both metrics her frequency is lower, the accuracy and success rates are quite high.

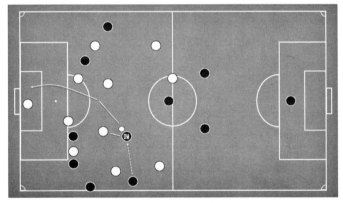

[FIGURE 32]

Many a time Marozsán has played against high-octane teams that will look to press Lyon's attacking players at every opportunity. *Figure 32* is a representation from Lyon's 2018 UEFA Women's Champions League game against Manchester City. Marozsán was able to create a shooting chance from an attacking throw-in. The German receives a quick throw from the full-back in the presence of two City players closing in. Her first thought is to take a touch away from her marker and take two touches towards the 18-yard box and shoot. This chance grazed the post, but it shows how perilous it is to allow someone of Marozsán's quality a chance to shoot.

Now, when it comes to Marozsán's off-the-ball work, you would think this is where she would struggle, but she plays an important part in Lyon's out-of-possession tactics. Lyon's press starts from the front, especially when facing teams who sit deep and attempt to play out from the back. Lyon often set up using a mid to low block, allowing teams to come out of their defensive third and attempt to win possession back in midfield. Lyon's 4-4-2 shape out of possession takes two forms – either a standard 4-4-2, or a midfield diamond – in which Marozsán takes up a spot as the second striker or attacking midfielder behind the front two. In both cases, she will look to press and harass opposing midfielders to force a mistake or even dispossess them, and look to play in the two quicker forwards.

Marozsán isn't the quickest, and by no means is she expected to perform at Kumagai's level with regards to her defensive duties, but there is an element of aggression to her movement as she works hard to comply with Jean-Luc Vasseur's defensive tactics and force mistakes out of the ball-carrier. For an attacking playmaker, her defensive statistics aren't as low as you'd expect. Marozsán averages 4.47 defensive duels (72.3 per cent success rate), 3.39 interceptions and 5.92 recoveries (83.6 per cent in the opposing half) per 90 minutes, which are quite high volumes. Marozsán's deceptive nature off the ball means opposing players may look to take their foot off the gas, which allows her that extra second to step in front of them or engage in a duel which results in a turnover.

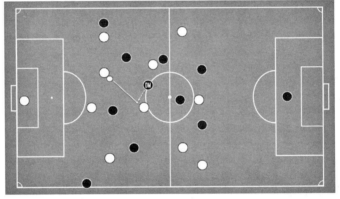

[FIGURE 33]

Taking a closer look at *Figure 33*, it gives us a clearer indication of how Marozsán's pressing comes into play. This has been taken from a game in last season's UWCL, once again against a team playing with a slightly higher defensive line but compressed spaces between the midfield and defensive lines. Here, Marozsán sees the pass is made to the player on her left and immediately looks to make a move across towards the ball-receiver. This pressing action results in the ball-carrier making a hurried decision rather than giving her time to pick the next pass.

The German international has been a key player for club and country for several years and, at 29 years of age, is still in her prime. While Lyon are preparing for the next generation, Marozsán will surely be part of the squad for years to come. She was close to an exit last summer to NWSL side Utah Royals, but a long discussion with Jean-Michel Aulas caused a change of heart and saw Marozsán pen a new long-term contract until 2023. Lyon's playmaker is one of a kind, and should rightly be considered as arguably the best attacking midfielder in women's football.

Chapter 11

Delphine Cascarino

*'The performance in the semi-final
and again in the final by [Delphine]
Cascarino was absolutely sensational.'* –
Sid Lowe

OF ALL players in the starting 11, you would have expected a Wendie Renard or Amandine Henry to garner such praise, but it was Delphine Cascarino who stole the show in the UEFA Women's Champions League Final against Wolfsburg in 2019/20. Cascarino is one of Olympique Lyon's brightest young players and she has been a sparkling star in a constellation of a team full of experience, icons and superstars. A team like Olympique Lyon are known for their decisive recruitment but also their empowerment of youth. Wendie Renard is a prime example of this policy and Cascarino is their next big product. The young French forward has played an integral part in the team's setup throughout the years, contributing to their success in their quests for both domestic and continental silverware. Having represented France from Under-16 level all the way to the senior squad, she has a wealth of experience for someone so young. Cascarino possesses one of the most important qualities needed in a team like Lyon, and that is a winner's mentality, having won the World Cup with France at Under-17 level and European Championship at Under-19 level. She's already made 73 appearances for Lyon, and still has a lot of room to develop the potential she has shown since bursting on to the scene.

Having joined the French club in 2009, aged 12, Cascarino has risen through the ranks and become a key player for the side under the different managers in charge. The 23-year-old started playing football for her local youth teams AS Saint-Priest and A.S. Manissieux Saint-Priest before joining Olympique Lyon along with her twin sister Estelle Cascarino. While her twin opted to move to Paris FC in 2016, Delphine was given a chance to show her talents in the first team having debuted in the 2014/15 season, and has not looked back since.

The importance of having a player come up from such an early age makes Olympique Lyon an attractive destination for young players. Their recruitment style changed slightly with younger names coming in, a prime example being 21-year-old Ellie Carpenter, who was brought in last season to replace the outgoing Lucy Bronze. Next, it's time to explain, and give you a better understanding of, what makes Delphine Cascarino unique and why she's been integral to the team's success.

At first glance, Cascarino's role resembles that of a traditional winger that uses the touchline and sends in crosses for strikers in the box. There is a modern element to her playing style, however, as she doesn't solely rely on overlapping movements, but rather is unpredictable in being able to drift out wide or come inside to create space and provide a different crossing angle or shot on goal. Her off-the-ball movement is equally as impressive as her on-the-ball skill, and this sort of profile gives

[FIGURE 34]

Olympique Lyon a different tactical weapon. The heat map in *Figure 34* (on page 123) is an indicator of where she often positions on the pitch, which shows heavy activity in the wide-right area, mirroring her role as a traditional wide winger.

To better place Cascarino's strengths, it is important to first understand the system and role she is played under. Lyon rely on their superiority in possession to ensure they keep the opposition as far away from their goal as possible. Cascarino plays on the right side of the three attackers that play behind talismanic forward Ada Hegerberg.

Olympique Lyon's attacking line-up consists of a number of dynamic and mobile forwards in Cascarino, Dzsenifer Marozsán, Amel Majri and Eugénie Le Sommer – four players who interact intelligently with Hegerberg. The 2018 Women's Ballon d'Or winner is mobile and intelligent in her movement, and able to get on the end of both aerial and low whipped crosses, making use of Olympique Lyon's different profile of wingers. Because of their aggressive and possession-hungry style, the full-backs are usually pushed up high and play close to their wingers. Both wide pairings will interchange positions between wide and narrow positions seamlessly with similar output, as both are equally proficient at crossing and ball progression.

Taking a closer look at Cascarino in possession, she is an aggressive, hard-working winger with particularly excellent crossing and dribbling abilities. Her high number of offensive duels is an indicator of her determination to protect and get past players while in possession. Combined with her pace, this could also indicate her ability in attacking one v one situations, where she is able to get the better of her marker and put herself in a better position to cross. What this also could indicate is her ability to create space in transition where she becomes the focus of defenders while she's on the ball. Her pace and dribbling down the line forces opposing full-backs to focus on her movement, leaving possible gaps between the centre-back and full-back for another player to exploit, whether it be Marozsán or Hegerberg.

Cascarino combines her pace, intelligent positioning and movement off the ball to also create space and allow her right-back, Lucy Bronze, to make overlapping runs and present herself as another passing option.

The pass map in *Figure 35* (on page 132) is a perfect illustration of Lyon's attacking structure against Stade de Reims, where Selma Bacha (number four) and Bronze (number two) (she is located under the number 23) are both positioned near the halfway line, with Cascarino (number 20) ahead of Bronze. There were

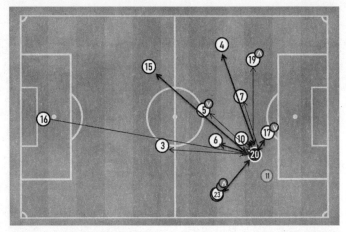

[FIGURE 35]

17 passes between Bronze and Cascarino, showing their connection and Cascarino's ability to develop a partnership with her full-back. This method of ball progression has made Olympique Lyon a massive threat and is why they've scored 67 goals this season.

Cascarino's main attributes include her understanding of space, which can be identified through her movement and positioning both on and off the ball. Her ability to drive past players using her pace, dribbling and crossing output is a result of this, which makes her so devastating against mid and deep blocks.

Starting with her in-possession traits, one of Cascarino's strongest assets is her dribbling which you can see just from looking at her statistics. She averages 10.72 dribbles per 90 minutes with a 61 per cent success rate this season. That alone illustrates her ability to progress play with such regularity, and her ability in taking players on through her high success rate.

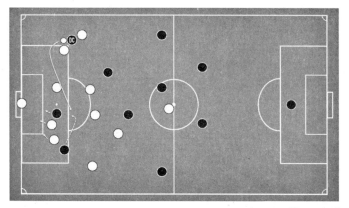

[*FIGURE 36*]

Figure 36 illustrates an example of her dribbling and crossing ability combined, where Cascarino starts off slightly farther back and is faced with the opposing winger and full-back. From here, her priority is to find a teammate with an intelligent cross, whether it be through a pull-back or a cross into the so-called 'corridor of uncertainty'. What makes this cross good, though, is the forward-thinking nature of it.

The cross is aimed for the vacant space behind the centre-forward with the left-winger coming in from behind. In this case, the left-winger makes a smart sudden turn towards the circled space that results in a goal. The forward movement by the striker takes the three players away, allowing the winger a free shot towards goal. Cascarino could very easily have played her cross in front of the defenders, but it could also very easily have been intercepted. She's able to take on multiple players at close quarters and still possesses the ball control to cross it into a dangerous area.

Another important part of Cascarino's game is the link-up play she offers to her team from a wide-right position. Vasseur's setup sees the team constantly moving, and is predicated on positional movements forcing every player to be comfortable in all phases.

Cascarino is another player that is able to contribute to this by dropping deep and moving inside to receive the ball and keep possession moving. Her ability to understand her position in relation to her teammates is good, with every move made knowing there is a player to fill in behind her.

At first glance, Cascarino's skill set seems ideally suited towards being a more attacking winger than an intricate, passing playmaker. However, while she is better going forward, her understanding of space makes for a simple passing game. During most games, you can find Cascarino dropping into midfield to receive possession from a central or attacking midfielder, with Bronze taking up the vacated wide area. These movements are intended to move opposing players out of position to create space in the original position.

Looking more closely at this passage of play from the 2019/20 UEFA Women's Champions League quarter-final against Bayern Munich, there is an interplay in motion in *Figure 37*.

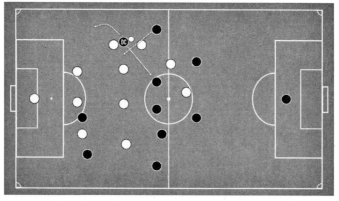

[FIGURE 37]

Cascarino receives a pass from a deeply positioned Marozsán in the right half-space, dragging her marker (the full-back) and possibly forcing the nearest midfielder to come in. Cascarino passes the ball back to Marozsán who has moved up, while Bronze makes an inside run.

During this move, Cascarino has moved back to her customary wide-right position and is now in a position to overlap the opposing full-back with the focus on Bronze and Marozsán.

Later in this chapter, there will be more detail on her off-the-ball understanding; however, this is just an indication of her footballing intelligence and how she can contribute to Lyon's link-up play.

What is also most pertinent here is her relationship with the full-back, specifically Bronze. As has been alluded to already, Olympique Lyon's system is reliant on every player's ability to interchange and understand their positions on the pitch, and this concept is no less important here.

While there are other options for Olympique Lyon in this position, the understanding between Bronze and Cascarino since the England international's arrival has seen an excellent understanding of where each other are on the pitch, which has contributed to numerous goals.

Their playing styles complement each other well, with both players equally comfortable playing in both a narrow or wide area, seamlessly interchanging positions, as seen in *Figure 37* (on page 135).

Some of Cascarino's qualities have been seen in off-the-ball movements through her link-up play, but she is equally proficient at moving into spaces to get on the end of passes forward. Often wingers are reliant on their on-the-ball abilities to create play, but Cascarino is able to create space by identifying spaces to run into, forcing the opposition to react by having a marker follow her.

Numerous times throughout this chapter examples of Cascarino's intelligence in and out of possession are on show and after reviewing her capabilities on the field, it is clear to see why she thrives at Olympique Lyon.

Figure 38 is an example of a situation where Cascarino can predict moves and makes early strides towards getting into position to receive. Here, she is situated in a narrower position, with the ball-carrier on the touchline. Cascarino identifies the space in behind the full-back and aims to capitalise on the movement made by the centre-forward who drags the centre-back away, opening up a path for her to run into. A darting run into the vacant space sees Cascarino latch on to the pass with her pace, allowing her to get away from the two players in front of her. Her starting position behind the two opposing players, where her pace can put her out of sight, is an advantage with them ball

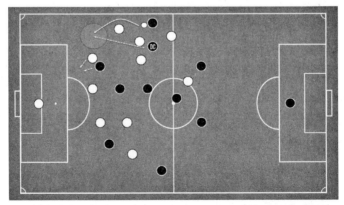

[*FIGURE 38*]

watching. It's this sort of intelligent movement that makes her such an asset to the team and follows the ethos of the type of players Olympique Lyon look to recruit.

Knowing that Olympique Lyon's defensive system is predicated on the whole team's equal involvement rather than that of a select few, it means the forwards need to contribute defensively too. Starting from the front, the team has a systematic way of pressing and defending and Cascarino plays an important part in this. She is not considered a very technically proficient defender, but her awareness, speed and hard-working nature ensures that she gets to the right place at the right time. Cascarino's most proficient skill in defending is her aggressiveness and willingness to pursue the ball-carrier.

The team transforms into a 4-4-2 off the ball when defending where Cascarino will hold her position in line with the second bank of four and adjust her position based on the ball's position. She is a solid presence on the right-hand side and provides Bronze with stable support against quick opposition wingers and full-backs. If Bronze is tucked into a narrower position or is in a slightly higher position, then Cascarino can be found filling in and stalling until Bronze gets back into position. Many teams will try to hit Olympique Lyon on the counter-attack, so having pace on the wings with the wingers dropping back to support the right-back becomes extremely important.

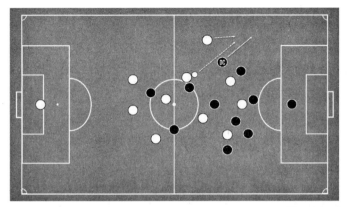

[FIGURE 39]

Looking at this example in *Figure 39* taken from a defensive situation in the 2019/20 UEFA Women's Champions League quarter-final, Lyon are being counter-attacked with Bayern Munich's left side completely vacant. Bronze has tucked in to cover the space Buchanan vacated when she stepped into midfield.

This means Cascarino needs to cover Bronze's right-back position. Due to the nature of the counter-attack, Cascarino understands that she must beat former Lyon full-back, Carolin Simon, to the vacant right-back position to either intercept the ball or occupy the full-back until Olympique Lyon's defence can reorganise themselves.

Cascarino has bags of potential and is someone that could improve any side in the world, not least Olympique Lyon. Having been at the club since she was a teenager, Cascarino's rise through the ranks has been remarkable. The winger still has lots to learn and improve, especially with her senior international career still in its infancy.

Cascarino's playing style is one that gives the team a different point of attack which boosts Vasseur's options up the pitch. In the long term, her future lies at right-wing, but Cascarino has the attributes to play as a centre-forward and an inside-left forward, which would make her extremely versatile.

For Cascarino, the goal is to cement her place as the undisputed number one and strive to fulfil her immense potential and continue to be part of Olympique Lyon's sustained success. The club have started to think about the future given last season's moves for Carpenter and Sakina Karchaoui, which marked a new wave of talent coming in. Cascarino will and should be part of the next wave of players going forward. She has all the talent to become a world-class forward for Olympique Lyon for years to come.

Chapter 12

Amel Majri

'Amel Majri dazzles with the ball at her
feet, bursting with energy and creativity.'
– Arianna Scavetti

'NEVER GIVE up.' A cliché that is commonly used to motivate and inspire people across many walks of life. It's also one used by Amel Majri in an interview she did in 2019 for *Onze Mondial*. It perfectly describes her journey to becoming a fundamental part of the most successful women's football team on the planet. In that interview, she also talked about her growing reputation, humble beginnings and, most importantly, what football meant to her. What's important to take away from this chapter is that the qualities Majri displays on the pitch are reminiscent of her life off the pitch. A quiet, reserved talent, she works tirelessly for the team and gets on with her job. Like worker bees who have dedicated their lives to protecting and serving the queen bee, Majri has similar qualities. In this case, the queen bee is Lyon and Majri is the worker bee; however, calling Majri a simple worker bee would be doing her a disservice, since she is more than just a hard grafter but rather a talented midfielder who has been at the centre of the team's success. Majri has been a silent operator in a Lyon team full of superstars that have come and gone – Alex Morgan, Megan Rapinoe and Lucy Bronze to name a few – remaining a constant presence who has consistently performed out of her skin year after year, game after game. So, who is Amel Majri?

Majri was born in Monastir, Tunisia, along with her twin sister Rachida. Having moved to Vénissieux at the age of one, both sisters discovered their love for football while vacationing in her native Tunisia thanks to their uncle introducing them both to the game, and from there a fiery passion for the beautiful game was born. However, they were restricted from joining an academy early on due to poor financial stability. The family couldn't afford to send both daughters, but the decision was made to send Amel to AS Minguettes. A football career was never on the horizon at a young age because she never thought it was possible, and it was only when she signed for Lyon as a teenager that she realised it was something she wanted. Majri joined Olympique Lyon at 14 and signed her professional contract at 18. After that, everything has unfolded and she has blossomed.

Like any mother, Hafsia Majri was afraid of her daughter playing with boys but she slowly recognised the talent unfolding in front of her. Having been so supportive of her daughter, it's painful to think that she isn't around to see Amel finish out her career after passing away a few years ago. Hafsia Majri was proud and happy, and used to tell everyone around her: 'This is my daughter.' Never one to put pressure on her children getting exemplary grades at school, her mother still wanted her to have a good level of education by completing her *baccalauréat* (a French national academic qualification received upon completing secondary school).

Majri's humble beginnings are reflected in her reserved persona, which stems from her desire for a private life away from the limelight. She is vehemently passionate about her goal to carry out humanitarian work in Africa, providing children with the tools to succeed, and wants to use football as a means to an end. To use the fame that comes with being a French footballing star is a humbling quality seen in a rare few individuals at the top of the game. It's projects like these that enrich Majri's reputation and make her a such an impressive and likeable character today. Taking all this into consideration, you can see why Majri has transformed into a serial winner and how these qualities shine through on the pitch.

Amel Majri is a jack of all trades rather than a specialist in her play. Throughout her Lyon career, Majri has played in several different positions, ranging from left-back to central midfield. The French-Tunisian midfielder has been a solid and consistent performer in every position she's played in, giving Lyon so many tactical options. Starting out her career at left-back, Majri was an attack-minded, marauding full-back that pushed on at will, providing an additional attacking option from deep, especially in the teams that she has been part of over the years that were strong, possession-hungry and fast.

Even for France, she played left-back and formed an excellent partnership with club teammate Eugénie Le Sommer in the 2019 Women's World Cup. An excellent player in possession with proficient technical ability and a high work ethic out of possession, Majri is a manager's dream. She's the sort of player that's required to carry out the hard graft to allow the more creative players room to thrive and succeed. Nowadays, Majri is mainly deployed either as a left-winger or left-sided central midfielder, but her role remains relatively the same.

Majri is a hybrid complete pressing central midfielder whose primary role is to win back possession and supplement the more attacking forwards by applying pressure on the opposition midfielders and defenders. A player in her position is tasked with playing a sort of box-to-box role and fill in wherever she is required on the pitch, which matches well with Lyon's positional rotations. Her proficiency in this role comes from her main strengths, which include spatial awareness, defensive positioning and ability to play under pressure. These attributes stem from her time playing at left-back, which contribute to the defensive side of her game. From an attacking perspective, Majri is an excellent ball progressor with her dribbling and crossing traits that give her team an added source of support. When she does play through the middle, Majri possesses a proficient quality of passing that's better than the average central midfielder but perhaps not quite at the level of a top-class creative player.

Putting these traits together produces a player that has been a mainstay in a Lyon team that harvests numerous amounts of highly technical and creative players. Getting the balance right between ball-winners, progressors and pure goalscorers is important, and Majri provides that. Being able to play in different positions at a high level enables her to translate those qualities into any position she's played in, which then elevates the whole team.

Similar players have been seen in other championship-winning teams, such as Chelsea Women's Sophie Ingle who was integral to their 2019/20 title-winning season, which contained a number of creative, attacking players in Sam Kerr, Bethany England, Guro Reiten and Ji So-yun. Similarly, N'Golo Kanté was a core part of Leicester City's and Chelsea's runs to the title in 2015/16 and 2016/17, where he played a key role in ball-winning, progression and just his sheer athleticism alone that ensured both teams were given a platform to win games. Majri's impact can be compared to that of Kanté's, where she covers every inch of grass and works tirelessly for the team. While Kanté is a more 'seek and destroy' sort of midfielder, and lacks precision in the attacking third, Majri has the added bonus of being better on the ball with good delivery, so there is a bit more contribution in that regard.

Lyon played multiple formations throughout the 2019/20 season, in which Majri has played in two positions: left-wing and left central midfield. The fluidity of the team means that she may start in a certain position, but her placement and movement are not rigidly fixed, and will more often than not end up rotating. In both positions, Majri will switch between attack and midfield, filling in gaps where the team requires her to be. During the league campaign, Majri mainly played as a left-winger that drifted centrally, but also played in the half-space to create different movement patterns to provide the attacking midfielder and left-back with space to attack and move. Since she's played in so many positions, I will explore Majri's strengths by examining how she's brought the different qualities from all her playing positions to the one she was used in during the 2019/20 season. I'll explain how she fits into the tactical setup from their 2019/20 campaign to provide better context to the aforementioned attributes and what makes her such a vital asset.

Arguably, where Majri's contributions have been most pertinent is her work off the ball, especially in the last couple of seasons. Being converted into a more central, pressurising midfielder meant a change in the way she went about her game. The transfers of left-backs Alex Greenwood (and later Sakina Karchaoui) and the emergence of Selma Bacha meant Majri was allowed to play in her more natural attacking left-wing position, but the addition of Nikita Parris and the extreme improvements of Delphine Cascarino meant Majri needed to accommodate these attacking players. This was done by moving her into a more central role, even if she started on the left wing. In doing so, Majri was able to cover more ground and take up more meaningful positions across the more active areas of the pitch. Being able to win back possession slightly higher up the pitch and force the opposition to decide their next move meant there were good chances of counter-attacks. She is one of the few players that doesn't have a major hand in build-up (except for when she's played at left-back) so most of her work only occurs in the second and third phases of play.

The basis of Majri's out-of-possession game centres on her movement, but most importantly her positioning. Being able to predict and place herself in a position that she knows will give her the best chance of recovering possession is extremely important. Positioning varies by role but Majri knows the space she vacates will be occupied by another player, so it becomes a lot easier for her to move freely. The positional rotations discussed earlier show how the team understand their roles and Majri is able to press and position herself in a systematic fashion because of it. Majri averaged 3.43 interceptions per 90 minutes in the 2019/20 season, which highlights her positional play from a midfield position. Her out-of-possession work differs in attacking and defensive phases. In

the attacking phase, it's more about pressing, while
in a defensive setting it's more about stopping the
opposition from getting through to the defence. Both
tasks are predicated on good positioning because,
without it, she's unable to carry them out diligently.

Let's start with how she operates in a defensive
scenario. Assuming Lyon start off in a 4-3-3 formation
and Majri is at left-wing when the opposition is on the
ball, she will look to play in the interior channels and
try and stop the team from playing centrally. This also
adds numerical superiority to Lyon's midfield which
ensures there is sufficient cover in all thirds.

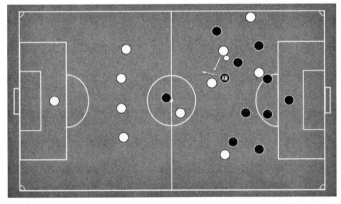

[FIGURE 40]

The illustration in *Figure 40* is a representation of Majri's
excellent out-of-possession work against Stade de Reims
in Division 1 Féminine. Majri initially has started in a
much higher position but has retreated as the team are

being attacked. You can see the compact and disciplined shape adopted by the team with Majri and Dzsenifier Marozsán (on Majri's right) forming a line of defence in front of them. The ball-carrier is looking for an opening and has one player free on the far side.

Majri identifies this and moves to block the passing lane before the pass is made. She is successful in doing so and puts Lyon on a counter-attack. Being able to predict and stop these sorts of passes is the difference between conceding a chance, and counter-attacking and creating a goalscoring opportunity for the team. This anticipation and ability to understand where to position herself in a defensive capacity comes from her time playing as a left-back. Though she was a very attack-minded full-back, the necessary defensive skills were honed and improved upon when playing against

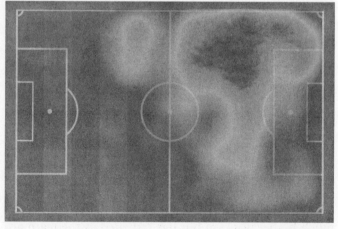

[FIGURE 41]

all types of opposition, especially teams from the UEFA Women's Champions League.

Figure 41 (opposite) illustrates Majri's heat map where her active areas are clearly highlighted. From the left flank to a more central position, Majri manages to move everywhere. Moving from the side to the central area means that not only does she provide support on the ball, but most likely off the ball too. What's also interesting is Majri's activity goes beyond the attacking areas and into her defensive third, which supports the notion of her box-to-box role. Being able to support an attacking full-back like Karchaoui means the two can play in tandem. Majri's performance of this sort of defensive role forms the basis of her defensive work. As has been mentioned, her stint at left-back was vital in becoming a better defender which has also translated to her defensive skills farther forward.

When she moved farther up the pitch, Majri could express herself more freely without having to worry too much about defending behind her. Though she still tracks back and helps her full-back, the tendency is to attack first and defend second. Looking at her statistics from the 2019/20 season, she averaged 5.15 defensive duels (66 per cent success rate), 7.13 recoveries (76 per cent in the opposition half) and 2.51 loose-ball duels (47 per cent success rate). All three statistics highlight her defensive capabilities and what's impressive to see is her high success rates, especially in loose-ball duels, of which she manages to win almost half. The 76 per cent of recoveries in the opposition half also indicates her pressing tendencies in the middle and final third. Majri is still able to balance her attacking qualities with her defensive intelligence in the higher areas of the pitch where she's able to close down opposition defenders and turn over possession, as in the case in *Figure 3*.

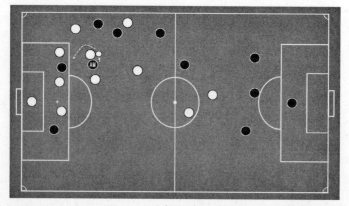

[*FIGURE 42*]

Figure 42 represents a moment that shows Majri's high-pressing style. Stade de Reims are trying to play their way out after winning back possession, with passing options forward. Majri engages in a duel against the defender and manages to put enough pressure on to win back the ball and ultimately win a free kick. This kind of commitment and work ethic is only seen in some attacking players and shows how important it is to have someone in this mould in a team.

Majri is not just active out of possession but is equally proficient in it. Being such a dynamic presence in midfield, her previous role as a left-back meant she was a very potent asset on the ball going forward on every occasion with direct ball progression and dangerous delivery. Even playing as a midfielder, she still uses these traits as a means to try and create goalscoring chances for the team when possible. Because she's able to win back possession in dangerous areas, there are times when Majri can play a through ball or cross, which will put someone through on goal or play in someone who is in a better position to play the final ball. As alluded to in this chapter, Majri's off-the-ball role is to move between positions to win back possession. Similarly, she takes up identical positions to perform the same actions going forward. Many a time you'll see Majri occupy the half-space and play in crosses, or drive into the interior channels to play through balls to any runners into the box. This combination works well with players like Marozsán or Amandine Henry who are both willing midfield runners and like getting into the opposition area.

So, what makes Majri such a formidable attacking player? It comes down to three main attributes: her range of delivery, dribbling and control in tight spaces. These traits are the basis of her attacking qualities and have come from her playing time as a left-back. You'll have noticed that there are constant references to her time as a defender because it's what shaped her qualities as a player now. Majri is both a connector and creator, switching between both roles as and when the team needs her to. Because of this versatility, she fits into a variety of tactical systems which allows the coach to manipulate the team and prepare for any type of opposition.

Starting with her range of delivery, Majri has a lethal left foot that has provided several assists over the years. As of October 2020, Majri had registered 26 assists in the league and Champions League since 2016 in 5,424 minutes. Looking at those statistics from an expected assists (xA)-against-assists perspective, Majri registered 0.43 assists across five seasons with an xA of 0.34. The French-Tunisian midfielder has outperformed her expected assists, which means she's been able to generate high-quality chances for her teammates, and the 0.43 assists shows the deadliness of the Lyon forwards being able to finish said chances. So, how good is her delivery?

Majri's first instinct is to find a forward pass or cross. Just as *Figure 43* shows, Majri is in a situation

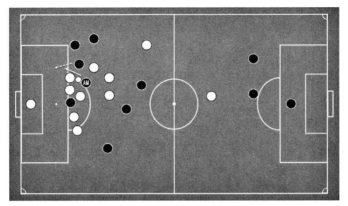

[FIGURE 43]

where she's picked up the ball high up the pitch, but is then surrounded by numerous defenders as she gets closer to the box. A lot of players in this position would possibly lose possession because of the pressure applied, but Majri takes half a second to play an acute pass down her right to play in the centre-forward. This pass creates a clear goalscoring chance because of the vast amount of space available with all the defenders focused on defending the central areas.

Her 5.94 passes to the penalty area (52 per cent success rate) and 1.52 through balls per 90 minutes are indicative of her skill. She frequently makes these sorts of passes when she's in a position to, which is an added asset to the team. Even when it comes to crossing, Majri is a very capable provider from wider and deeper areas. The combination of her dribbling and crossing out on the left flank is much feared by opposing full-backs because of her directness and precision. With an aesthetically deceptive dribbling style, many defenders might think they have a chance to win back the ball. More often than not, though, Majri is able to drive forward and use large spaces intelligently.

Majri works in tight spaces, and similarly when she's put under pressure, she is able to keep hold of the ball and deliver the final pass. Her 4.69 dribbles and 4.56 crosses per 90 minutes is quite high given she starts off in a more central position. Both statistics have over 40 per cent accuracy rates, which gives the data much more context.

Being able to constantly get into crossing areas and deliver in a team that is often faced against deep, compact teams is impressive.

The illustration in *Figure 44* (opposite) shows Majri in a situation where she needs to drive in behind the opposition defence to make use of the space. She's faced up against the full-back in a one v one position where she engages in the duel and uses her strength to muscle her way past and deliver in a cross to the far post. Majri's aggression on the ball is noticeable and it is what makes her such a direct threat in the wide areas.

Majri's overall contribution to the team is extremely valuable and effective. Being one of the hard workers in

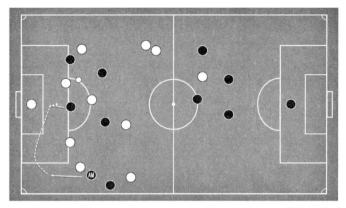

[FIGURE 44]

the team, her contributions to Lyon over the years have
been vital, with her ability to play in multiple different
positions where she's performed diligently. Starting
out as a left-back and moving to left-wing gave the
team a natural attacking look to their left flank, but
when required, she has moved across to a more central
midfield position, especially in the absence of Henry
during the 2019/20 Champions League run when she
had to adapt to the position and curb her attacking
instincts slightly.

However, she was able to convert herself into a
promising pressing central midfielder by taking up a
'seek and destroy' role that would break down and start
attacks and, if the opportunity arose, create chances.
The French-Tunisian midfielder is one to keep her head
down and not garner too much attention; this is how she

thrives in the team. The likes of Hegerberg and Eugénie Le Sommer add star power to the team, so players like Majri can thrive in the shadows.

Chapter 13

Amandine Henry

'Amandine Henry is a force unto herself in midfield. She can overpower opponents defensively just as well as she can pick out a pinpoint pass to contribute offensively.' – Arianna Scavetti

LEADER. IT'S one of those roles that needs a certain type of personality and one which only a few have truly been able to carry out. Every team sport needs their leaders – people who will lift the dressing room when the chips are down, and step up and inspire their teammates when their backs are against the wall. In every successful team, you'll always see more than just the captain taking on a leadership role. Chelsea's 2004 and 2010 teams had Branislav Ivanović, John Terry, Frank Lampard, Didier Drogba, Michael Ballack, Petr

Čech and Michael Essien, who were all part of a Double-winning side. Liverpool's 2005 UEFA Champions League winners included Steven Gerrard and Jamie Carragher, while Arsenal's 'Invincible' season was driven by Thierry Henry, Patrick Vieira and Martin Keown.

Each of these sides were winners, serial winners in some cases, and like them Lyon are all about trophies and titles. What they also have are leaders. Though Wendie Renard is club captain, the side is filled with players who are standout personalities on and off the pitch. Amandine Henry is one of them. Captain of the French national team, Henry is a big voice and presence in the dressing room and is one who has inspired Lyon to title after title. Surrounded by big-game players, Henry isn't one to back down and has stood out to become arguably the best defensive midfielder in world football. The road to being recognised as one of the world's best required sacrifice and dedication to excel in her craft. Henry's tale starts out like other girls who dream of a career in football growing up, playing with the boys in order to fulfil her passion. Until the age of 13 she did just that, but she didn't just play – she shone.

At 15, she joined Hénin-Beaumont and continued to showcase her talents. In her inaugural season, as a defensive midfielder no less, she hit the back of the net 11 times in just 20 appearances. From there, she's never looked back. A good two-year spell caught the attention of Olympique Lyonnais and, at 17, she started her love story with the French champions. Her ability to excel in every department comes from her playing in Europe and the United States. Henry had a spell with the Portland Thorns, which she credits with toughening up her physical game.

Since her stint in the US, she's played for Paris Saint-Germain before returning back to Lyon. However, it's safe to say that she left the best for last; her latest stint at Lyon has yielded some of the best football she's played and contributed to an important period in the club's history. Henry has won 26 titles with Lyon since 2007, making her one of the most successful footballers to grace the game. Individual accolades haven't escaped her either, but it's little wonder why she's considered one of the best and why she's been so integral to Lyon's sustained success over the years.

Henry's role in midfield is a demanding one that requires more than just being a good passer or runner. Capable of playing as a central or defensive midfielder, Henry is one of a rare breed of midfielders who are adept at both the attacking and defensive phase of the game. Henry is usually paired as part of a double-pivot or three-man midfield and acts as both a connector and a driving force. Her role is essentially box-to-box midfielder, which she typically carries out from a defensive midfield position in a two-man midfield alongside Saki Kumagai. Henry is responsible for playmaking from deep through the build-up phase, but also in the middle and final thirds.

Henry's box-to-box role sees her involved in all phases of play. Her primary playmaking responsibility is to connect midfield, defence and attack, which she is able to do thanks to her excellent ball-carrying skills and vision. From dropping deep and collecting possession from the centre-backs to playing through balls into the strikers, she is exceptional in her positional awareness wherever she is on the pitch. Off the ball, Henry is tasked with making late runs into the box to act as an extra body to support the attacking players, while also contributing defensively by covering positions vacated by other players.

What's made her so successful over the years is her ability to execute this role with diligent consistency. Henry is essentially the team's quarterback who can make plays but heavily contribute to other areas too. She provides support to the forwards during attacks, helps with playmaking, and her positioning aids the defensive structure of the side as well as providing support and protection to the defence during opposition build-up. Henry's main strengths lie in her vision, creativity, and positional and spatial awareness, which contribute to her actions across the phases of play. Exceptionally talented in passing, dribbling and under pressure, you'll be hard-pressed to find a real weakness in her game.

Being the team's fundamental link player, Henry is often just seen supporting players while still being involved as a constant presence, whether it be out wide with the full-back or centrally next to the central defenders. She is the player that ensures that Saki Kumagai is well supported defensively and simultaneously supports Dzsenifer Marozsán when it comes to creating chances. If she isn't doing either, you'll find Henry making precisely timed runs into the box to score important goals.

It's hard to compare Henry's style of play to another single player because her quality reflects that of numerous talents around. She is in some ways a one-of-a-kind player in women's football, with no one else really coming close to her skill set. American midfielder Lindsay Horan is regularly touted as one of the best midfielders in women's football and could be the only real comparison. However, if you take a look at the men's game Marco Verratti of Paris Saint-Germain is a player who shares similar qualities and has the same desired effect on his team. Both Verratti and Henry are extremely important to the way their teams play and their presence changes the way they can operate.

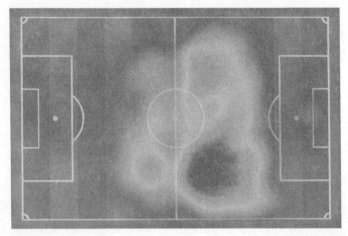

[FIGURE 45]

Figure 45 is Henry's heat map and it supports a lot of what has been discussed already. Playing on the right side, most of her hotspots are situated in and around the halfway point, but she has a presence across the central areas too. Though most of her activity is in the final third rather than the defensive third, you can see that Henry plays as a box-to-box midfielder, with the majority of her attacking and defending work done in the right half-space. It is here where she can use her effective passing and aggressively press teams high. Henry is such a dynamic midfielder that it comes as no surprise that she covers so much of the pitch.

Playing alongside Kumagai in the double-pivot, Henry will be in different positions depending on where the ball is. I'll explain Henry's role as a defensive midfielder in all three phases of play both on and off the ball. Starting with the build-up phase, she is one of two passing options for the centre-backs to pass into as a way towards the full-backs. The full-backs are pushed up and the primary target during build-up, but if a direct passing option towards them isn't available, then Kumagai and Henry are always on hand. Henry will drift into a wide-right position to receive passes as she has a responsibility to take up Lucy Bronze's position when she moves forward. This is part of Lyon's positional rotation tactics that ensure numbers across the thirds. Both Henry and Kumagai are excellent under pressure, so chances of them being dispossessed in this area remain unlikely. Teams will usually sit off the centre-backs employing a mid-block, which is triggered when the ball is played into midfield. Once Henry is in possession, it is up to her to turn, drive and pass the ball out from Lyon's defensive third into the middle third towards the highly positioned full-backs or wingers. Henry will usually be in the same line as the two right-sided players, which gives her options to go down the line, inside or back towards the goalkeeper, though the latter option is rarely used.

Positioning is key for Henry and is the basis from which she builds her game. She always makes herself available to pick up the ball and isn't afraid to come deep, even if she's tracked by an opposing player. Being able to pick up possession from her defensive midfield area and move it towards the halfway point through passing or dribbling makes her one of the best at this. Henry is a proficient passer and is equally adept at dribbling – one of the reasons she is a trusted player in build-up – while being such a composed player on the ball helps considerably. Her ability to shield the ball is an undervalued trait, but one that not only helps in build-up but that also creates space farther up the pitch as it forces the opposing team to commit players into pressing her.

Now, let's analyse each of her traits a little closer. First, looking at her passing range, Henry more often than not will use short, simple passes to progress the ball, but is equally comfortable taking a riskier approach by playing long, grounded, direct passes into the forward players if the opportunity presents itself. Being a player with the vision to spot passes from deep, Henry is not afraid to try and play in the quicker forwards who are more than capable of running in behind or dropping into pockets of space to play off a nearby player.

Figure 46 is an illustration of Henry's role in build-up which infuses her passing and dribbling in one. This

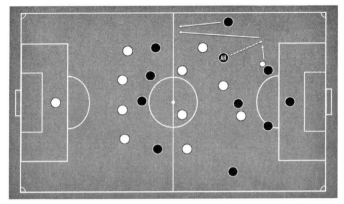

[FIGURE 46]

example shows Henry's movements and positions while showcasing her ability to read the situation to better gauge progression. Here, Henry drops into Bronze's position as the right-back starts to bomb forward. That foray forward triggers Henry to move towards the position to receive the pass from the centre-back. From here, she takes the initiative and drives forward, given that she sees an opportunity to push forward with no players nearby. This in turn allows her team to get farther up the pitch than a simple short pass to her nearest teammate would.

Her build-up role tells only half the story. Henry displays most of her strengths farther up the pitch because it is here where she can showcase her abilities on the ball. Part of her task in possession in midfield is to ensure constant ball rotation and forward movement.

Making sure Lyon are advancing the ball forwards is of utmost importance and it is up to Henry to provide a base from which the team can propel themselves forward. She will look to find one of the wide players or Marozsán before making her way forward into a more attacking position, but only once she's sure a turnover is unlikely. As I mentioned already, her job is to act as a connector rather than be the team's creative fulcrum. Her positional awareness is what is key here because it's this that enables Henry to pick the right pass or know where to be when the ball goes out wide to get on the end of a pull-back or cross from the edge of the box.

Henry being partnered with a counterbalance in midfield plays an important role. Being set up with Kumagai is part of the reason why she's so effective in the middle and final thirds. The duo balance each other out. When one is more defensive-minded, the other is a more attacking presence. Their understanding is such that they are rarely seen far apart from one another, ensuring they provide cover for each other. Part of Henry's intelligence comes from knowing if her teammates are stationed in good positions to support her attacking forays. This propels Henry to position herself to create attacking opportunities and control the tempo of the game by scanning the field even from an initial defensive position. Henry has been deployed in a similar role for France too, and is paired with a Kumagai-esque player.

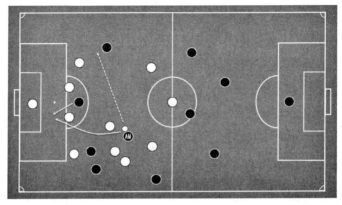

[FIGURE 47]

Being able to quickly assess and understand in-game situations and make right decisions is a very difficult skill and one that is almost innate. Henry is a naturally gifted footballer, but what makes her even more special is the tactical mind she possesses. *Figure 47* showcases this in an example taken when she was on international duty with France. Henry steps up into the left channel with her teammate being closed down by three opposition players. The interior pass comes towards her with Henry keeping one eye on the players in and around the box. There are two players making runs on the far side (Valérie Gauvin in the box and Kadidiatou Diani on the far side) which gives Henry an idea. While it isn't visible in this illustration, Henry feigns a pass towards Diani who is farthest away but actually slides a disguised through ball for Gauvin in the 18-yard box, all while being closed down. Given the quick pace of the game, Henry's swift reactions meant France were able to penetrate the opposition's sturdy defensive line and get a shot away. She isn't fazed by much, and given her experience, it's hard to envision a better ball-carrying midfielder in Europe.

The numbers speak for themselves. Her 2019/20 season statistics (taken from Division 1 Féminine and the UEFA Women's Champions League) show a clear pattern. Henry averaged 61.98 passes (87.4 per cent accuracy rate), 46.27 received passes, 13.88 passes to the final third (79.8 per cent accuracy rate) and 21.05 forward passes (78.6 per cent accuracy rate). These numbers suggest that Henry is very much an influence on the ball, especially when it comes to passing. The high accuracy rates along with her high frequency means that she's at the centre of Lyon's transitions from defence to attack. Forty-six received passes is another indication that play runs through the French international, though given the level of competition in the league and initial stages of the UWCL, some numbers might be inflated. Having said that, this shouldn't take away from the fact that Henry is an influential figure next to Kumagai in midfield.

Besides having a good passing ability, Henry is a very capable ball-carrier and is another source of ball progression in the final third where she can bounce off teammates in quick exchanges and push forward with her driving runs. Her 3.32 progressive runs and 2.41 dribbles per 90 with a 65 per cent success rate is exemplary for a player that plays in a deeper midfield position, though is expected for the role she occupies. Lyon's right side already had two excellent dribblers in Bronze and Cascarino, who are both exceptionally talented attacking players, and Henry's supporting role means she can provide the unexpected outlet. What stands out is her 5.41 offensive duels with a close to 50 per cent win rate, which shows that she is someone who can keep the ball and won't lose it easily.

Henry's ability to create space for her teammates around her is another added by-product of her dribbling.

In *Figure 48* (page 172), Henry's first thought is to push into the composed backline which shifts the focus on her. The result of this means that at least one player benefits from being left unmarked – in this case it was the left-winger. Henry drives far enough to then pass it out wide and continue her run in behind to either get on to a return pass or see the ball get crossed into the box.

There have been examples of Henry's abilities in an attacking and transitional sense with her on-the-

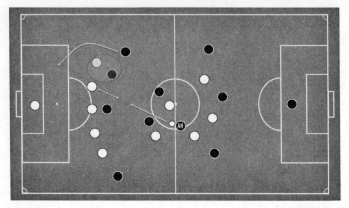

[FIGURE 48]

ball skills, but she is equally effective off the ball too. Usually, once she plays the ball into another attacker, she'll find a position in the zone attacking midfielders usually occupy to assess if and when she needs to make a run into the 18-yard box. This is to ensure she is able to cover in midfield and prevent counter-attacks. Being the intelligent player that she is, Henry is a player that knows her limits and, even though she isn't a massive goal threat, she has contributed so much to the way Lyon score their goals, but has also made a crucial impact defensively.

Henry's defensive role is to ensure that she covers any out-of-position players on her side. While this is a team tactic rather than an individual instruction, Henry is mainly tasked with covering any advancing players, particularly the right-sided full-back, Bronze. Usually in build-up, Henry will shift into Bronze's position while she pushes and builds up out from the back. It's not only a ball progression method but also a way of insuring any loss of possession farther forward.

If Lyon do lose the ball in midfield and are faced with a counter-attack, Henry effectively becomes the team's right-back until Bronze can recover. Even when Bronze moves back into position, Henry will hover around the half-space to ensure numerical superiority and a pressing body. It's her spatial understanding that allows her to move into different positions to cover and temporarily become a second holding midfielder akin to Kumagai. This transformative quality is what makes her such an imperative player in Lyon's setup.

It's not only having spatial awareness that automatically makes her a good defensive midfielder. Being in good positions makes her job of defending much easier and, more often than not, she's successful. Interceptions and defensive duels are her main defensive actions of choice. The ability to predict where passes will go is a very good trait which stops the opposition putting undue pressure on Lyon. If she's able to stop a through ball or block a long ball over the top, then not only does it thwart the attack, but it also gives other players time to get back into position in case the second ball is won back by the opposing team.

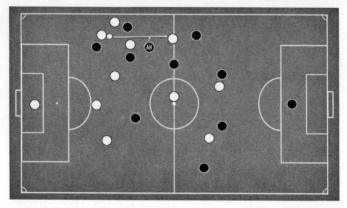

[FIGURE 49]

Henry always looks to assess situations as quickly as possible and eliminate imminent threats smartly. In *Figure 49*, you can see that Henry's first instinct is to cut the passing lane before it gets in behind Lyon's defensive line. Henry's starting position is at right-back where she's covering for Bronze. Her instinct to move into this position means that she's able to cover while the opposition have won possession and are looking to play over the top. Henry has understood the danger and looks to nullify it by moving in front of the ball to intercept. This is also reflected in her 4.82 interceptions, which highlight her importance in this role and her good initial positioning.

When it comes to direct engagements, Henry isn't one to back down. Part of being a box-to-box midfielder means the player needs to be able to defend well and win back possession to initiate a turnover. Because of the positional rotations of this Lyon team, someone like Henry can press opposition midfielders without exposing her position. Having the presence of mind to know when to press and when to hold back is only borne of tactically intelligent players, of which Henry is certainly one. It's no easy task playing as a central defensive midfielder, especially one that plays in a team that is expected to dominate possession and must be wary of opposition sides counter-attacking at any given moment. Again, the numbers are quite telling in this regard, where Henry has 5.41 defensive duels (67.5 per cent won), 4.3 aerial duels (65.2 per cent won) and 9.71 recoveries (73.8 per cent in the opposition half). What you immediately notice is Henry's high win percentage rate, which coincides with her excellent positioning that is at the centre of it all. Seventy-three per cent of her recoveries in the opposition half comes from Lyon's high defensive line and their willingness to win back possession higher up the pitch.

Some of the better-quality teams will look to try and build out from the back and attempt to play through Lyon's press. Due to Lyon's mid-block pressing structure, any time the ball enters the middle third, it triggers Henry, along with Marozsán, to start pressing their counterparts.

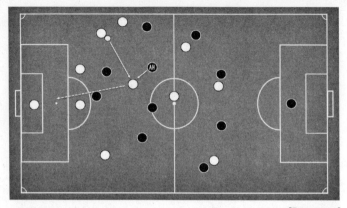

[*FIGURE 50*]

In *Figure 50*, you see Henry closing down the sole defensive midfielder and force them back towards their goalkeeper. Henry has been such a useful player for Lyon in defensive situations that the only way they could find sufficient cover for her was by signing the Icelandic midfielder Sara Björk Gunnarsdóttir, who is considered in the top five in her position.

Amandine Henry is a figure of leadership, experience and everything that Lyon have become in the last decade. Though she only rejoined Lyon in 2018, Henry has been typical of the way Lyon have conducted their transfer business and the profiles they aim to bring to the club. Bringing back a player of her quality for a second stint typifies their need and desire to continue finding excellence. Henry exudes this in abundance, and the class and quality she displays with every touch, pass and run has yielded trophies in every season she's been at the club. Entering her 30s, Henry still has a few more years of top-level football to give and has already cemented her place in Lyon folklore. With a new generation of talent coming through, Henry will be responsible for mentoring her future replacements and ensuring the Lyon dynasty continues.

Chapter 14

Lucy Bronze

'No one works harder than Lucy Bronze,
and no one matches her for toughness.' –
Arianna Scavetti

LUCY BRONZE has played football from a very early
age, but it could have been very different if it had not
been for her own hard work and determination. Being
one of England's best players and winning numerous
titles playing for the champions of England and France
wasn't even a dream for Bronze, mainly because she never
thought it was ever possible. For her, it was all about
playing the game she loved, even for free, just as long as
she kicked a ball. Bronze grew up loving sports – not just
football – and playing with her brother and his friends'
team, which was where she got her kicks from. At the age
of ten, Bronze was banned from playing with the boys'

team but was encouraged to keep playing because of her innate talent. Running around empty fields with her dog and using staircases to keep her fitness levels up was how she maintained herself, but this never deterred her from playing the game she loved.

'Growing up, it wasn't the dream [to be professional] – the dream was to always play football whether I got paid to do it or not.' – Lucy Bronze (*Give Me Sport*)

Bronze has had her fair share of setbacks, having gone through four knee surgeries to the point where she visited a sports psychologist because she 'couldn't run'. She revealed some startling news in an interview with BBC Sport. The first injury came during her first training session with the England Under-19s where she made contact with the ground which snapped her knee in half. After visiting a surgeon, she was told: 'You need to have surgery now otherwise you might lose your leg. It's infected.' It was not something you want to hear after an injury like that, although the most brutal part of this story is when her Under-19s manager called and harshly told her she wasn't going to get picked.

'"You're not going to be fit enough to play this summer. We've got a World Cup and a Euros. We're

*not picking you to play. Bye." He just put the phone
down. That's when I was left to my own devices.
I didn't have a physio, so I used to go to the park
with my dog and just run laps. That was me for
three months, training as hard as I could to get fit.'*
– Lucy Bronze

Bronze's career hasn't been smooth sailing, but she
has now has become one the best players in women's
football, and arguably the best in her position. The
England right-back has worked her way up to the top
of the ladder; securing a move to Olympique Lyon was
the pinnacle of her career, given they are arguably the
best team in women's football history.

The England international has been a revelation,
going through a number of clubs before eventually
signing for Manchester City in 2014. Having played
for Sunderland, Everton and Liverpool before signing
for City, Bronze has been a success wherever she's been.
At Liverpool, Bronze won the FA WSL in 2013 and
again in 2014, while at Manchester City she won the
FA WSL Cup.

Her impressive performances persuaded Lyon to
sign the England right-back, which presented her with
her most successful period of trophies, winning nine
titles in her three-year stint.

A whole host of individual accolades followed, including the PFA Women's Players' Player of the Year (twice) and BBC Women's Footballer of the Year (also twice). She was even recognised with the FIFA Women's World Cup Silver Ball and UEFA Women's Player of the Year Award in 2018/19, becoming the first English player to do so. It's fair to say that success has been associated with Bronze for most of her career, but what has made her such a vital part of Lyon's sustained success over the years? Coming to a prestigious club graced by stellar names meant there were high expectations for the right-back, but given the accomplishments and the work she'd put into making it so far, you'd have bet your house on her being a success.

Bronze's role as a right-back is as progressive as it gets. The modern full-back is expected to carry out both attacking and defensive duties equally well, given the demands of managers and tactics. Traditionally an attack-minded full-back, Bronze is able to diligently perform both an attacking and defensive role, such is the nature of her playing style. What makes her stand out from other full-backs is her ability to play both the inverted and attacking full-back roles so competently.

Bronze's main attributes revolve around her positional intelligence and spatial awareness which contribute towards her attacking and defensive positioning, enabling her to execute defensive and attacking actions. Her passing, dribbling and speed are three core traits that contribute to her attacking endeavours, while her tackling and tactical intelligence are part of her defensive repertoire. The combination of these traits and attributes is what makes Bronze arguably the world's best right-back.

Bronze is more akin to Kyle Walker, David Alaba and Philipp Lahm than Dani Alves, and while all three were under the tutelage of Pep Guardiola, they were schooled in different ways based on their strengths.

Bronze is involved in numerous roles for Lyon, from build-up to defensive transition structures and attacking support. Going forward, she provides Lyon with an outlet down the right-hand side, combining well with right-winger Delphine Cascarino. Having the ability to both underlap and overlap makes the combination play down Lyon's right flank much more unpredictable and dangerous. Comfortable in possession, Bronze is an excellent ball player and carrier which enables her to drive deep into the opposition half without being dispossessed when pushing teams back, which then affords the likes of Cascarino more space in the final third. If she doesn't foray forward, she uses her excellent range of passing, particularly her long passes which have been used to good effect in relieving pressure and switching play. A versatile player, Bronze is equally comfortable taking up a midfield role, as she has done on occasion for England, which explains her ball-playing calmness and precision.

Defensively, Bronze is very comfortable in taking on players in defensive situations, especially in one v one situations. Knowing her position and the players around her makes it much easier for her to control the situation and make the right defensive call. Part of Lyon's tactics involve a full-back tucking inside to become a tertiary centre-back, a role Bronze has filled many times. Her tactical nous enables her to switch from right-back to centre-back with ease and coordinate with her teammates.

In build-up, Lyon often look towards their full-backs as a way to progress forward from the centre-backs or defensive central midfielders, with Bronze being the main outlet. The central defenders and defensive midfielders look for a full-back to try and utilise the pace they have in the wings. This method of build-up gives Lyon space in midfield once play moves inside and allows the quick wide players to have an impact.

Bronze will sometimes act as an auxiliary midfielder due to her higher-than-normal positioning on the pitch. Lyon dominate possession over most teams, enabling the full-backs to play slightly higher up the pitch and enjoy much more freedom to join attacks. Nevertheless, they must still adhere to their roles at both ends of the pitch. If one full-back pushes forward, the other must be slightly deeper to ensure numerical advantage in midfield, defence or both.

This section will start off by analysing Bronze's role in build-up and how she plays an integral part for Lyon. Their aim when playing from the back is to progress the ball from the wide areas to the central striker. The idea is to eventually use the half-spaces and put in whipped crosses or cutbacks to play in the centre-forward. Kumagai and Henry are where Lyon look to operate most of their initial distribution, whether it's through the first or second pass into the Japanese international. When Kumagai is in possession, she will find her defensive midfield partner or one of the full-backs, even if it means playing a series of short and simple passes that will eventually open up small gaps to progress play forward. This will eventually allow the full-back to push forward in attacking areas because the centre-backs and defensive midfielders have invited the opposition to press them.

The quick transition into Bronze then allows her to burst forward at pace and play in Cascarino and Dzsenifer Marozsán. What allows Bronze to initially take up these higher positions is the positional rotations of the defensive midfielders. Mainly through Amandine Henry or Sara Björk, one of them will drop into the right-back position which triggers Bronze to push forward. When the ball reaches Henry/Sara Björk from Kumagai or the centre-back, they will look to play down the line towards Bronze, who in turn will either drive forward on the overlap or underlap and pass it on to one of the attackers.

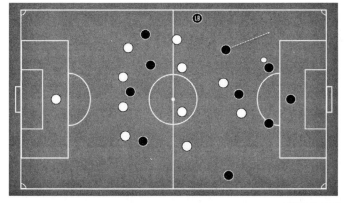

[FIGURE 51]

Figure 51 is an illustration from the 2019/20 UEFA Women's Champions League Final where Bronze can be seen in a higher position as Lyon start playing out from the back. Sara Björk slots into the right-back position and her first instinct is to find Bronze and start an attack down the right-hand side. Björk will then join the attack and create a numerical advantage in the middle third, with Cascarino dropping deep to provide a passing option. It's in these positions that Bronze is able to threaten much more and is able to help Lyon build out from the back. While Lyon's left side undertakes this too, both Sakina Karchoaui and Selma Bacha are more supportive wide players supplementing the attacking Eugénie Le Sommer and Amel Majri. This isn't to say that they don't attack in general, though, as Lyon look to use the same tactics on this flank too when the chance presents itself.

So, from Bronze's role in build-up, it is clear that her biggest impact is in the forward areas where she spends most of her time. Both in transition and attacking moves, Bronze has a big influence on how Lyon are able to transition forward and attack from the wide areas. Once one of Henry or Kumagai finds Bronze on the wing, she uses her speed and dribbling to drive down the flank and force opposing teams to put their focus on that side of the pitch. Being able to carry the ball at speed with very good footwork means that pressure is taken off the central players and it creates more space in midfield. In Marozsán they have a number ten that tends to move around in her attacking midfield area and is excellent at finding spaces to receive the ball in any way, but giving her even more time to receive a pass after a marauding Bronze run means that she can do more damage.

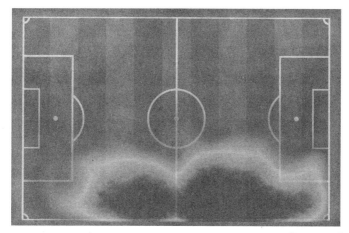

[FIGURE 52]

As has already been mentioned, Bronze's usual position is higher up the pitch, which coincides with Lyon's high defensive line; what this means is that Bronze will have a bigger impact in the final third. *Figure 52* is indicative of her activity across the right-hand side of the pitch. You can see how her heat map has most of her activity in the final third, with some internal movement in the area too. I will explain the effect her attacking moves have on the players around her in the next example, but it's important to know how effective her dribbling is to this.

A lot of attacking right-backs need to be powerful and quick when dribbling forward, which is what Bronze brings to the team. Not too many teams can boast a player of this quality, other than perhaps Chelsea's

Maren Mjelde, who can be considered a more defensive full-back, or Bayern Munich, who have a more attack-minded full-back in Hanna Glas. Bronze averages 4.79 dribbles per 90 minutes with a 67.8 per cent success rate, which is very impressive considering that almost every team Lyon come up against are set up to be a lot more compact.

Having looked at Bronze's role in build-up and knowing how she manages to help progress possession for Lyon, this moves us on to the next phase of her possession-based skills, which is her movement and decision-making in the final third. In this space, Bronze really showcases her intelligence in play. She has the ability to make quick decisions which is needed in Lyon's fast-paced attacking style. Whether it's choosing between an underlapping or overlapping off-the-run ball, or driving inside when the opportunity arises, Bronze is more often than not able to make the right choice.

Making these decisions is based on the opposition's setup and her teammates' positions within the area. If Cascarino is seen on the outside but there is a better position to pass from, Bronze will drive inside, inevitably attracting players her way to allow Cascarino a lot more space to receive the ball unopposed and create a clear chance to cross or pass. She is very explosive and this becomes much more potent in smaller spaces because of her ability to push past players. Bronze is so good at this that, in fact, she ranked first in the UWCL rankings for one v one dribbling in the 2019/20 edition of the tournament with a 75 per cent success rate. The English right-back also ranked tenth for progressive runs which, considering the tactics employed against her, is not too terrible.

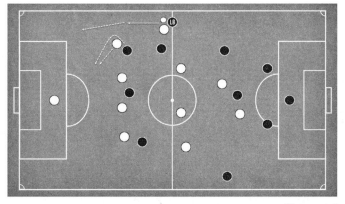

[FIGURE 53]

Taken from the game against Wolfsburg last season, *Figure 53* demonstrates Bronze's dribbling and decision-making abilities in one example. Bronze is faced by Dominique Janssen who she manages to get ahead of by knocking the ball past. From here, the right-back was able to anticipate teammate Sara Björk's intention of moving inside and reacted by continuing her run. Most importantly, not only did she get the ball farther up the pitch in a better crossing position, but it diverted the attention of the two closest Wolfsburg defenders, thus leaving Sara Björk with more space to receive the pass from Bronze in the box.

A player like Cascarino is extremely quick and smart with her movements on and off the ball, and the relationship the pair have developed has shown on the pitch. Cascarino is equally comfortable drifting inside or staying wide, which makes the interchange with Bronze much more unpredictable for opposition defenders. Both are explosive with their dribbling and movement, so it's little wonder that Lyon focus their attacking intentions so much down the right flank.

Another important weapon in Bronze's arsenal is her passing ability. While her short passing is good, it is her long progressive passing attribute that truly makes her a standout player. A lot of the time, you'll see this Lyon team play passes between the back four, looking for an opening with many teams staying compact. Bronze is one of Lyon's main passing outlets from the back with her trademark long cross-field pass into the left-winger or attacking left-back that switches play and diverts attention to another part of the pitch.

The idea behind this is to try and open up space on the right side by making the opposition shift across to the opposite flank. In doing so, space opens up for the right-sided attackers, while Bronze assumes her defensive responsibilities in midfield. From a statistical point of view, she has been solid. Looking at the 2019/20 season rankings in the UWCL, Bronze ranked first for progressive passes with 94 throughout the tournament. It's no coincidence that Lyon's right-back is a major source of their progression from the wider areas and has been able to effectively create the groundwork for her midfield teammates to find final-third openings.

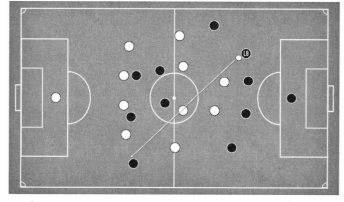

[FIGURE 54]

Figure 54 is a representation of Bronze's passing range and ability to switch play to create an opening. Here you can see her coming up against a disciplined and structured midfield and defence which is set up in a low block, meaning the midfielders and attackers are marked. Bronze uses this chance to switch play to the left side where her teammate is in some space and will quickly push forward, trying to disrupt the opposition's shape. The England right-back averages 3.41 long passes with a 53.2 per cent success rate, which compared favourably to some other top right-backs. Maren Mjelde of Chelsea averaged 2.38 (51.1 per cent) and Hanna Glas of Bayern Munich (formerly of Paris Saint-Germain) averaged 2.3 (52.9 per cent). These numbers, along with her showing in last season's Champions League, is a testament to her ability to find ways to progress the ball.

The other side of any full-back's game is their defending, which is vitally important to the role. Bronze's role in Lyon's system is interesting and tactically different from a lot of right-backs in world football. In the earlier chapter on Lyon's defensive structure, there were details about how the full-backs are a major part of the team's way of defending, not only in one v one battles in the wide areas, but also as part of a faux back three and midfield cover. Bronze will switch between defending against opposing wingers and full-backs to tucking inside to become part of a back three alongside the two centre-backs.

Depending on the midfield shape at the time, Bronze will even tuck into midfield and become another layer of protection if the defensive midfielder drops in between the two centre-backs to fill in the gap there. For Lyon, it's always about having numerical superiority in each line through positional rotations, and the use of the full-backs makes this possible. This is where the Guardiola influence comes in his use of Alaba, Lahm and Walker. The 'inverted' full-back has become such a clever way of covering two different areas, ensuring there is enough cover while maintaining superiority.

One may ask, what makes Bronze such a versatile right-back individually? Well, most of her defensive traits revolve around her positional awareness and speed, leading to plenty of interceptions and clearances which can result in turnovers. Astute defensive positioning allows her to stop players attacking, and for the most part, not let them get past her. When she does engage in these defensive duels, Bronze focuses on trying to isolate the player to keep them as far away from goal as possible. This involves her being positionally aware, and of course being a very good one v one defender. The next example will explain how she uses these traits in her defensive role as a whole.

Being so tactically adept comes from Bronze's high footballing IQ. The ability to move from position to position requires intelligence, good positioning and speed – Bronze possesses all three. Jean-Luc Vasseur wanted to take advantage of these traits and use Bronze as a multifunctional defender playing in defence and midfield, utilising her pace and aggressiveness off the ball. When Bronze drifts into midfield, she's able to press and track down opposing ball-carriers while having the cover of three defenders behind her. Similarly, when she plays in a back three, Bronze can stop central attacks or push out to help the winger if needed.

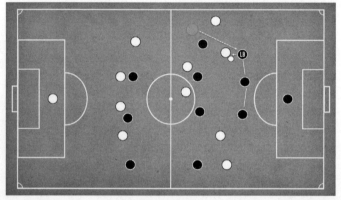

[*FIGURE 55*]

Taken from a game against Paris Saint-Germain in the 2019/20 season where Lyon are building an attack, *Figure 55* illustrates Bronze in a defensive situation where she's moved into a central position. An interception in the middle by PSG triggers Lyon to quickly form a back three. They pack numbers around the ball-carrier and receiver, but what is also prevalent is the positional rotations occurring again. Bronze makes her way back from a higher position on the right to become the third centre-back and disrupts Marie-Antoinette Katoto from receiving the ball.

Part of the reason for Bronze playing this role is her ability to read the game so well. If you look at the numbers, they reflect her ability in a defensive capacity. Bronze averaged 5.67 interceptions, 12.98 recoveries (51.7 per cent in the opposition half) and 6.44 defensive duels engaged per 90 minutes. The right-back's number for interceptions is very high and indicates how often she manages to anticipate these moves from her position, wherever she may be. To further emphasise this, in the 2019/20 UWCL, Bronze ranked first in interceptions with 45.

Lucy Bronze has been an integral part of Lyon's history and team successes over her three years at the club. No other defender has shown her level of consistency and output and they will have certainly missed her after her move to Manchester City at the start of the 2020/21 season. A theme that repeats itself throughout this book is that Lyon have regularly signed or developed only the very best talent in their positions, and there is no doubt Lyon had that in Bronze. She is a living testament that success is possible in women's football, especially in a period when it was much harder to break through without all the riches of the modern era. But as she says: 'These things we call sacrifices are never really sacrifices if you love what you do.'

Chapter 15

Ada Hegerberg

*'When the spotlights are brightest and
the pressure is on, Ada shines brightest.
She demands the ball and delivers in the
biggest moments.' – Arianna Scavetti*

MOST FANS will have heard of the name Ada Hegerberg. This is mostly because of the number of records she's set over the years, and the fact that she has arguably been the best player – or at least the best centre-forward – in women's football over the last few years. For those that haven't, Hegerberg is a mercurial striker who has not only scored over 300 career goals with 53 in the UEFA Women's Champions League – making her the current all-time top scorer – but has also won the inaugural and coveted Ballon d'Or Féminin, five

UEFA Women's Champions Leagues and six Division 1 Féminine titles, all by the age of 25. You'd be forgiven for thinking these accolades belong to a player in the twilight of their career but it's quite the opposite. The team's talisman, Hegerberg has been at the forefront of the success that Lyon have earned over the last few years, but it isn't just what she's accomplished on the pitch that has garnered so much attention.

The fight for equality in women's football is an ongoing battle and one that is being led by the few influential superstars like Marta and Megan Rapinoe. Hegerberg herself has made sacrifices in her own way to continue the fight by opting out of playing for the Norwegian national team after a dispute with the Norwegian Federation. Though the finer details have not come to light, in an interview with *The Telegraph* she cited 'inequality of opportunities for girls and women in the sport' in Norway as the underlying reasons. The 2019 FIFA Women's World Cup felt Hegerberg's absence, and though the tournament was considered a rousing success, it would have felt complete if the Nordic striker had been present. Brazilian superstar Marta, arguably the greatest women's player of all time, talked about the importance of the collective and Hegerberg's stance on the matter in an interview she did for *Omnisport.*

'*When I talk about gender equality, I think that all women that can talk about it, they are allowed to talk also. What I mean is that Ada is paying a price of not playing for her country but this fight of hers is a fight of all of us.*' – Marta

Hegerberg has had a relatively injury-free and consistent career thus far. However, an anterior cruciate ligament injury to her knee in January 2019 was the first time she had sustained any kind of long-term injury, but it came at a time when the world was put on hold. In an interview with CNN, she talked about the rehab process, her feelings about the injury and what she did with the extra time away from the pitch. With a love for learning, she found a new perspective watching sports documentaries. One that she watched was *The Last Dance*, a ten-part docuseries, which follows Michael Jordan's final season with the Chicago Bulls. While she doesn't compare herself to the legendary player, Hegerberg found one moment particularly poignant.

'*When he talks about the fact that it's lonely at the top and got emotional at the end of one episode ... It really got me because I really understood what he meant. I invest everything into football every day in order to perform.*' – Ada Hegerberg

The 'investment' she talks about shows in her competitiveness on the pitch and the fight she shows when playing. She oozes class and a special aura that only top-class players command. You can watch a passage of play with Hegerberg in full flow and instantly understand the level of quality she possesses and that is embodied in this Lyon side.

Fighting for titles on the pitch and equality off it, Hegerberg is a modern-day superstar and the closest the women's game has to a Ronaldo or Messi. Though she lacks an adversary, Hegerberg is well and truly a one-of-a-kind striker. The coronavirus pandemic hasn't helped and Hegerberg has issued a rallying cry for the authorities to take care of the women's game for it to continue flourishing on the back of a successful 18 months. All of this just adds to the Norwegian's persona of being a determined, no-nonsense serial winner. What you see on the pitch translates to her work off it and much more.

Hegerberg is an elite-level centre-forward and one who possesses many capabilities in the final third. While she is primarily in the team to score goals, her role as a striker goes beyond that. Her qualities are unrivalled in some departments with proficiency both on and off the ball. Many strikers in women's football tend to float in and around the box and are more inclined to find space in the box, with the elite strikers capable of being part of more than one phase of play. Samantha Kerr is an excellent link player and finisher, while Marie-Antoinette Katoto regularly drifts into the channels and has an eye for goal. Hegerberg is arguably a level above in terms of her all-round play. In some quarters, she is considered the best striker in women's football, and it's hard to argue because the numbers are astonishing; she regularly scores 20-plus goals a season, especially in the latter stages of tournaments.

As a complete striker who can compete and influence play both in and out of the box, Hegerberg's role for Lyon is an all-round one. From dropping into the channels to getting on the end of crosses, she is very aware of her surroundings and is a lethal finisher. Spearheading the attack, Hegerberg is able to play with a variety of different profiles of players around her, which is one reason for her success in this position. Being able to get on the end of high crosses or through balls, her ability to judge and understand game situations is like no other.

On the ball, Hegerberg makes direct runs at opposition defences with her excellent dribbling ability and is not afraid to take a shot from distance. If there's an opportunity to play in a teammate, then Hegerberg will not refrain from making that pass. Her vision and range of passing in the final third are phenomenal for a striker and the reason for Lyon's fluidity in this area. Off the ball, she's intelligent enough to understand the space around her and is regularly seen dropping into the channels or deeper positions to pick up possession and drive forward.

This not only gives her team a source of progression, but also someone who is adept at holding up the ball and making time for runners such as Amandine Henry or Eugénie Le Sommer to make direct runs into space. Defenders are afraid of leaving the Norwegian striker free because of the damage she can cause, so more often than not she'll pull players out of position. She even provides plenty of aggression which is a huge asset for Lyon's defending off the ball that starts from the front.

These traits perfectly describe Hegerberg on the pitch with her qualities for all to see. All of Lyon's free-flowing football needs a reliable and clinical outlet, which she provides. She has a way of bringing in other players and giving them space to work in the final third, which brings an unpredictability to her game. All in all, Hegerberg's strengths lie in her vision, creativity, spatial awareness and goalscoring ability. She knows where the goal is and manages to find the back of the net better than most strikers. It would be fair to say that Hegerberg's style is very much like Harry Kane of

Tottenham Hotspur. The Spurs striker is the heartbeat of the English side's attacking endeavours and has slowly transformed into a creator as well as a goalscorer. His link-up play and finishing ability is deadly and is reminiscent of Hegerberg's style. The Norwegian centre-forward has a similar effect on Lyon.

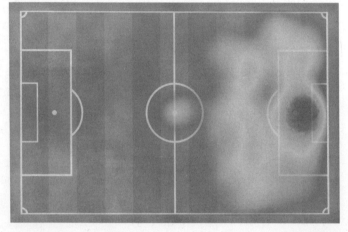

[FIGURE 56]

Playing as the main, central striker she's not one to stray too wide but rather focuses on vertical movements more than horizontal ones. Being able to play in between the lines and going as far as the half-space, Hegerberg has developed relations with the wingers and attacking midfielder to be able to create more passing exchanges. If you look at *Figure 56*, you can see where Hegerberg's activity is on the pitch. Naturally, the most active areas are in the middle of the 18-yard box, while her activity in and around the box, especially in the half-spaces, is evident. This supports our description of Hegerberg's style of play and her tendencies to drop and link up play. Throughout the book, you've seen how involved the players are in build-up from the central midfielders to the full-backs, and even the forwards play a part. Hegerberg is not as involved in build-up but becomes active when the ball enters the final third. From here, she's able to move around and affect play through the aforementioned attributes.

So let's delve a bit deeper into the out-of-possession traits that make Hegerberg such an elite centre-forward. Arguably, the most important trait for a striker is their movement both in and out of possession – it can be the difference between a striker scoring ten and 20 goals a season. Understanding where the ball is going to be and where best to be positioned at the end of a pass or cross is vital because it allows the player to move away from defenders and make them unpredictable. A player like Hegerberg is reliant on her excellent movement to be able to both link play and create space for other players to run into.

Usually, when Hegerberg drops into spaces, it's to pick up possession and speed up play, which then starts to pull players out of position. Her 18.55 received passes may not be very high, but it's enough to show involvement in this area. Lyon have a number of different players who play around the Nordic striker. The likes of Dzsenifer Marozsán have the creative skill set to take advantage in smaller spaces playing behind her, so even the shortest of movements make the biggest differences. You've got excellent off-the-ball runners in Amandine Henry, Eugénie Le Sommer and Nikita Parris who are adept at finding space in the final third, so when Hegerberg drops into pockets of space, those players are able to take advantage.

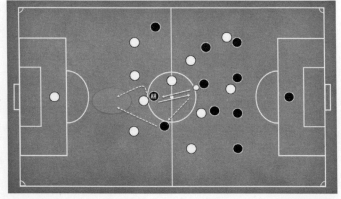

[FIGURE 57]

Taking the example from *Figure 57*, Hegerberg is up against a determined Bordeaux side trying to stop three Lyon attackers. For Lyon to penetrate through, they need to quicken the pace and pull players out of their compact shape. To do so, Hegerberg drops into space which prompts the central defender to come out with her and ensure she doesn't turn and put pressure on the striker. However, this movement not only pulls the centre-back out of position, but it forces the neighbouring full-back to make a choice whether to cover the vacated space or track the left-winger's run forward.

Hegerberg passes the ball back into midfield, which is then moved on to said left-winger. This series of passes is made quickly, enabling Lyon to find some joy down the flank to create a goalscoring opportunity. You can refer back to her heat map to see how much time she does indeed spend in the areas outside the box, which reflects her style of play.

Hegerberg is not only good at creating chances, but is equally adept at breaking the lines and finding space in the 18-yard box. The old adage 'fox in the box' is quite accurate in Hegerberg's case because of the burst of acceleration and intelligence she possesses when it comes to finding and timing these runs. Lyon have quick wingers and full-backs, especially Delphine Cascarino, who is problematic for full-backs on the right side. In the 2019/20 UEFA Women's Champions League Final, Cascarino was named player of the match for an electrifying display featuring her menacing runs and crosses.

This sort of service for a lethal finisher like Hegerberg is what she thrives on. It not only diverts attention away but allows strikers to get on the end of tap-ins. While Hegerberg is someone who can score a variety of goals, you can be assured that being able to score these so-called 'easier' chances is much more difficult than it looks simply because of the timing and gambling required to make these runs.

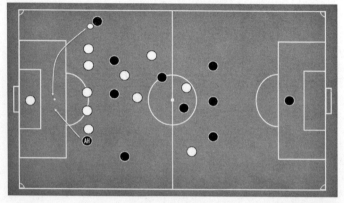

[FIGURE 58]

Figure 58 is an illustration of Hegerberg's off-the-ball movements when it comes to getting into goalscoring positions. The ball-carrier on the right is stretching the defence, with Hegerberg positioned on the shoulder of the last defender, waiting to make a run. Her instinct is to make a forward run towards the six-yard box the second she sees the cross come in. This Lyon team know each other very well, so understanding their tendencies becomes like clockwork and these types of runs become much easier.

The quality of the movement is also important here as Hegerberg doesn't just make a straight run, but rather makes a diagonal run to cut the angle and get to the ball quicker. Statistically speaking, in the 2019/20 season Hegerberg averaged 10.31 touches in the box and was even ranked first in the UEFA Women's Champions League for the same metric. Bearing in mind her season was cut short due to rupturing her anterior cruciate ligament in her knee in January 2019, the results are remarkable.

From a defensive aspect, Hegerberg does contribute to the press, which is where Lyon are so dangerous without the ball. The hard work put in by all the forwards is a cultural trait that's instilled in the Lyon players. While the majority of the battles are engaged in midfield, it is up front where the pressure begins. Off the ball, Lyon revert to a variation of a 4-4-2 where Hegerberg is partnered with one of the other forwards who will try to press the ball-carriers. The idea is to force a mistake and create a situation where a turnover can occur as high up the pitch as possible for Lyon to counter-attack. It is here that Hegerberg is able to duly apply enough pressure and initiate this press as the focal point of the team.

In possession is where the Norwegian striker is devastating and has garnered her reputation. Hegerberg is a pure predator with killer instincts, scoring goals for fun sometimes, though what is it about her skill set on the ball that makes her so dangerous? Well, it's a mixture of a few traits that have already been mentioned including dribbling, creativity, passing and finishing. All these traits overlap and coincide with each other to create the perfect storm. In a nutshell, Hegerberg is an adept ball-carrier who has the vision and creativity to pick out players around her, but also has the ability to capitalise on chances that present themselves.

Having so much of the ball means that there are times when there isn't space to dribble freely. However, as you've seen from her out-of-possession movements, Hegerberg is a player that drops into the channels to pick up possession and find space. These attributes contribute towards Hegerberg's playing style as it is predicated on her movement and positioning through dropping deep and linking play. This can lead to two results: after making runs into the channels, she either creates a shooting opportunity for herself, or she plays in an overlapping or underlapping runner before positioning herself in a goalscoring position in the box.

This is where her ball-playing intelligence comes to the fore. If there is a player in a better position, she will always look to find her to create the best possible chances. Strikers of her level are often selfish; they have to be in order to score goals and have the belief to finish off opportunities. However, Hegerberg is someone who's been able to act as both a provider and finisher. Her intelligence in decision-making and knowing which pass to choose makes her an exceptionally talented forward.

Using the Kane example from earlier, it is possible to be considered a top-class forward without constantly taking difficult chances. The England striker has regularly played deeper than strike partner Son Heung-min, with the two creating an excellent partnership. Marozsán, Le Sommer and Cascarino have all developed this sort of relationship with Hegerberg and can expertly navigate into pockets of space to receive passes off the striker. Just looking at her expected assists (xA) and assists from the 2019/20 season, she registered 0.24 assists per 90 minutes with an xA of 0.21, showing that the quality of chances Hegerberg produces is being converted into goals by her teammates.

In *Figure 59* (on page 210) you can see an illustration of Hegerberg's vision on the pitch. In this game against Paris Saint-Germain, Le Sommer makes a pass into Hegerberg who drops deep to receive the pass. The Parisian centre-back has followed the Norwegian striker and allowed Marozsán to make a run in behind. Hegerberg knows what her movement has done and, as a

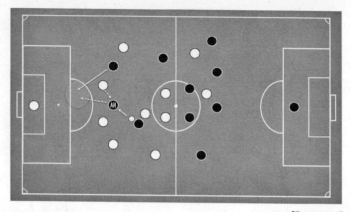

[FIGURE 59]

result, quickly turns and plays a through ball in behind the defensive line for the German playmaker to latch on to. The quick thinking between the three forwards created a goalscoring opportunity which combined Hegerberg's creative passing, Marozsán's off-the-ball movement and Le Sommer's initial quick pass.

From a statistical point of view, the centre-forward averages 3.14 passes to the penalty area with a 49 per cent success rate, which for a striker is quite high. To manage to successfully find a teammate with half of them is impressive, considering she's closely marked by central defenders in every game. In the UEFA Women's Champions League, she ranked first in expected goals and assists (xG + xA) with 9.12, which shows how frequent her contribution is to the team's overall style of play. Hegerberg even ranks fourth in deep completed passes (defined as a pass that is targeted to an area within 20 metres of the opponent's goal), which again highlights her importance here.

Hegerberg made her reputation based on her goalscoring exploits which stem from all the attributes discussed throughout this chapter. For one, Hegerberg broke the record and claimed the all-time goalscoring record in the UEFA Women's Champions League in October 2019 by scoring 50 goals in 53 appearances at the time. Since the 2015/16 season, no one has scored more goals than the Norwegian striker, with 48 in the competition.

Hegerberg makes goalscoring look easy and with her development rapidly increasing year on year, you'll find that she'll only get better. The striker has the capacity to score all types of goals from headers to 30-yard screamers but it's the technique and precision that she adds to her shots which makes her so clinical. Her movement, positioning and creativity are the main aspects of her game which all add up to her impeccable style and one that only comes with confidence and intelligence. Since she moved to Lyon in the summer of 2014, Hegerberg has been a revelation at the club and has epitomised the club's success over this dominant period.

Having won games and finals on her own at times, Hegerberg is on course to set records akin to Lionel

Messi and Cristiano Ronaldo. With age on her side and the women's game only getting better and more competitive, Hegerberg has the chance to stamp her authority on the game even more and prove she's the greatest of all time. Hegerberg and Lyon's success go hand in hand and it's no coincidence that they've both achieved so much together.

The executives, the players and the club are all on the same wavelength and follow the same ethos: winning. Having bred and identified players who operate on a similar level, they've been able to sustain this level of success. Any time their worth has been questioned, they've risen to the occasion. Much like her club, Hegerberg will thrive off competition and while they've proven their credentials as a European powerhouse, it will need the Norwegian to be on top of her game to lead the next generation of players once this cycle is over.

Chapter 16

The End of an Era?

AS THE referee blew the full-time whistle in San Sebastián, you could feel a sense of relief and joy in the atmosphere. The players celebrated their fifth consecutive UEFA Women's Champions League win in a deserted stadium but achieved the unimaginable. A lingering sense of doubt had hung over the Lyon side who silenced their critics as they ran out 3-1 winners. The players proved their worth at a time when they weren't at their best and Wolfsburg were seemingly at the height of their powers. You could see the distressed faces on the German team who felt this was their best chance to topple the French giants, but Lyon came out with a point to prove. They had an almost 'us against the world' mentality. Ninety minutes in Bilbao was another reminder to the world of what's made them the dominant European side in women's football.

* * *

People have thus witnessed the culmination of a project that's been ten years in the making, with Jean-Michel Aulas the driving force behind the scenes. From the acquisition to their latest Champions League victory, their success has come down to the president's vision and willingness to turn his women's team into an unstoppable force. With competent coaching and talented players, Lyon have had it all. The capital invested has been sustained for years, but most importantly the social support from Aulas and his team has been unparalleled. From private jets to matches and a modern training facility, Lyon's women's team enjoy the same privileges as their male counterparts. Even the bonuses were equal as Aulas paid the women the same as the men after their win against Paris Saint-Germain in the UEFA Women's Champions League.

All of this has catapulted them into stardom, making Lyon one of the most attractive destinations and the pinnacle of a player's career. The players they've invested in bringing to the club has expanded their reputation and prestige. Lucy Bronze, Nikita Parris and Sara Björk Gunnarsdóttir were highly sought after by the club, but equally there was a desire from the players who jumped at the chance to play for Lyon. The lure of playing alongside Ada Hegerberg, Amandine Henry and Eugénie Le Sommer can be irresistible. The opportunity to learn, train and play with three of the world's best isn't something that comes up every day. However, the murmurs of last season weren't without reason; the team did find themselves in a dip. Whether it was due to the pandemic break or lack of rhythm, Lyon were missing something.

> '*There was a sort of a feeling this year at the tournament, this was kind of the last time that the challenge to Lyon is growing and the five in a row was significant. Not because in European football history that means equalling Real Madrid, which is what you'd say is the benchmark.*
>
> *I think there was also a sense that this was the last time because there was a growing sense of a threat from other clubs, [especially with] the development of Barcelona and the growth of Real Madrid, if they continue to put the resources behind them, and the Women's Super League.*' – Sid Lowe

So the question remains, where does this team go from here? At the time of writing, Lyon have been beaten by a resurgent Paris Saint-Germain side, which put an end to their 80-game unbeaten streak stretching back to December 2016 where they lost to – fittingly enough – Paris Saint-Germain. There's been a feeling that the other European teams are closing the gap and it shows in the results. Bayern Munich are seriously challenging Wolfsburg and Paris Saint-Germain are in the running once again. Chelsea and Manchester City are slowly but surely hitting their strides, and have the squads to cause real damage in Europe. No club has ever sustained success forever, but Lyon looked close to invincible for the best part of ten years. Even Pep Guardiola's Barcelona side had their demise, so it's no shocking revelation if this team starts to decline.

The future of Olympique Lyon might be hazy to say the least, but they've undoubtedly set the standard and become the modus operandi for every women's football club aspiring to achieve greatness. Look at many clubs around the world, and you can see they are slowly replicating the model of the club both on and off the pitch, with improved investment in their playing squads and training facilities. The very top clubs are beginning to see the appeal women's football has around the world.

The success of the 2019 FIFA Women's World Cup was a significant catalyst in propelling interest and putting the very best on the biggest stage. Chelsea Women are a prime example of a team who have taken an approach that is similar to Lyon's model, but also one that is used by the men's side.

Aulas will act swiftly to rectify the situation if it doesn't improve by investing once again. The importance of refining a squad cannot be understated given the quality Lyon have had. At the time of writing, Lyon have been linked to Arsenal's Vivianne Miedema, Barcelona's Caroline Graham Hansen and Real Madrid's Sofia Jakobsson, bearing in mind that several key players have contracts running out in the summer of 2021, including Eugénie Le Sommer, Delphine Cascarino, Jéssica Silva, Amandine Henry, Saki Kumagai and Sakina Karchaoui. Hegerberg's early renewal means the priority contract renewal is complete, with a focuses on the rest. There is a school of thought, given the players in question that are soon out of contract, that Lyon could revitalise the squad with a more youthful look. Towards the end of the first half of the 2020/21 season, Lyon were giving more game time to their academy products, with some showing a lot of potential to thrive in the first team. Twenty-year-old Melvine Malard is one who seems to be on the verge of becoming a first-team regular, with others such as Sally Julini and Vicki Becho in and around the squad. Left-back Selma Bacha broke into the team in 2017 and has showcased glimpses of her immense talent which could finally convince the management to give her a proper go as the number one left-back.

Arguably, Lyon's biggest move came when they announced the signing of Catarina Macario from Stanford University in January 2020. She is considered one of the best prospects for the US women's national team in years. The young forward was tipped to be the number one draft pick in the NWSL College draft but chose to ply her trade abroad. The thought of her and Hegerberg terrorising and leading a new generation of Lyon players is an exciting prospect to say the least. This signing was a statement like no other, showing the world they can still attract the very best talent to France. Pair this with potential signings of Miedema and Jakobsson and Lyon could very well have the foundation for another decade of dominance, but there is little doubt that the summer of 2021 is vital to their long-term success. Every player, whether backup or indispensable starter, has played a part in their success and will be needed going forward, so future-proofing their squad in some capacity is a requirement.

At the start of the book, I talked about some of the greatest dynasties built by some truly great teams, and Lyon are certainly up there. I believe the future of the club is in the balance and it won't be as easy to reach the summit with a number of world-class teams emerging on the horizon. By the time you read this, you'll know who won the 2020/21 UEFA Women's Champions League and that will give you a clear idea about where this team is headed. A win propels them to an untouchable status that makes them a truly legendary club in women's football folklore. A loss doesn't necessarily dent their achievements, but it does slightly remove the fear factor, giving other clubs more confidence in being able to achieve what is considered as the Holy Grail in the subcontinent.

Will they continue to be at the pinnacle? That remains to be seen, but what is certain is these players have earned the right truly to be called the undisputed Queens of Europe.